Literature and Life

NCTE Committee on Classroom Practices in Teaching English

Literature and Life

Making Connections in the Classroom

Classroom Practices in Teaching English,
Vol. 25

Patricia Phelan, Editor,
and the Committee on Classroom Practices

National Council of Teachers of English
1111 Kenyon Road, Urbana, Illinois 61801

Cover Design: Carlton Bruett

Interior Design: Tom Kovacs for TGK Design

Staff Editor: Michelle Sanden Johlas

NCTE Stock Number: 29625-3020

Printed in the United States of America.

Library of Congress Catalog Card Number 85-644740

Contents

Preface

This year the Committee on Classroom Practices chose to issue a call for manuscripts that would help students "interact with literature and make it their own." We were concerned with successful classroom practices that encourage students to make connections between literature and their own lives, to encounter the richness of ideas and variety of values which authors past and present have shared with us.

After our November 1987 meeting, the call for manuscripts was issued in the major NCTE journals. By September 1, 1988, we had received seventy-eight manuscripts. These manuscripts, with authors' names removed, were evaluated by committee members Carlota Cárdenas de Dwyer, Beverly Busching, Nancy Broz, Kent Gill, and Jackie Proett—a committee representing several geographic areas and grade levels.

Twenty-eight manuscripts were finally selected and submitted to the NCTE Editorial Board for approval to publish. All the contributions represent exemplary classroom practices that enable students to connect literature and their own lives in a variety of ways. The committee hopes this volume will provide fresh ways of approaching literature at all grade levels, from kindergarten through college.

Introduction

The title of this volume presupposes that we place a high priority on helping students read fine literature and share their own experiences with those of the author. Rosenblatt says, "The reader brings to the work personality traits, memories of past events, present needs and preoccupations, a particular mood of the moment, and a particular physical condition" (1976, 30). As teachers, we believe that making connections is at the heart of real education. Of what use are an author's ideas if we cannot make our own meaning from them, test the ideas against our experience, and see how they relate to our picture of the world? In the classroom we work to help readers create their own "webs of meaning," free to encounter the literature in ways that are significant to them (see Corcoran's "spinning webs" [1988]). Susanne Langer's *Philosophy in a New Key* suggests both "discursive" and "presentational" modes of response in which students engage literature through language and through artistic, symbolic expression (1957, 79–102). In the process of teaching in this kind of classroom, we find our own relationship with literature renewed and changed in partnership with our students, a rich experience.

The practices offered here cover a wide range of classrooms, kindergarten through college. You will find that you can adapt ideas from all of the selections to fit your own students. For example, Morrissey offers a third-grade program in which partners read books and participate in response activities. Partners may read, research, join other partners to share ideas, and report back to the total group at any grade level. Mandel suggests the value of choosing an ambiguous text as the basis for literary study in college. What freedom of expression and fresh insights might result from the use of ambiguous text in a first-grade class as well? Livingston's dinner party, where students are the authors they have read, will be engaging across grade levels. Golub's suggestions for students to generate questions and respond to poetry are applicable in any classroom. As you read, notice ways you can "connect" with ideas from teachers representing a wide variety of classrooms and approaches to presenting literature.

Part I centers on students collaborating and creating meaning from what they read. Nolan introduces this volume with a central question for readers, "How did this book make you feel?" Smagorinsky's American literature course provides students with a literary framework for developing their own values. Such activities as sharing journals, debates, and dramatic presentations encourage students to seek meaning together. Cobb and Delia offer a Socratic approach to *Antigone* and to "Stopping by Woods on a Snowy Evening," respectively. Barron and Sosland ask students to grapple with moral dilemmas before they begin *Death of a Salesman.* Hamilton's classes design and create class banners of the books they read. The classroom practices in Part I have in common a response to literature involving collaborative activities and an integrated language arts approach.

In Part II, teachers suggest ways to help students connect with literature through more specific reading, listening, and writing strategies. Although there is a more specific focus in this section, you will discover that these ideas also represent an integrated approach. Jenseth shows how to help readers learn through rereading, understanding, and "enactment" of *Hiroshima.* Kutiper and Abrahamson offer research to show which modes of presenting poetry most appeal to junior high readers. McKendy uses an old multiple-choice test to improve students' reading and discussion of a work. Sherrill offers a poorly written story as a way into developing literary criticism. Clark's reading aloud to first-grade students leads them to listen in order to explore new places, people, and ideas, using all of their language skills. Turk shows students how to write pattern poems as response to setting, character, and conflict in the stories they read. Both Kelly and Christenbury suggest ways to create new text by freeing students to create their own versions of the literary masters they have read. Bean-Thompson concludes this section with a unique approach to critical writing, in which the writer begins with contradictions in the literature in order to arrive at a generalization, rather than starting with a bland general statement and then supporting it.

In a variety of classes at many different grade levels across the country today, students are making connections between their lives and the literature they read. To again echo Rosenblatt, "The literary work . . . is a mode of living" (1976, 278). We hope the exemplary classroom practices offered in this volume will help you to connect with your students and the literature you teach in new and refreshing ways.

Patricia Phelan
Crawford High School, San Diego, California

References

Corcoran, Bill. 1988. Spiders, Surgeons, and Anxious Aliens: Three Classroom Allies. *English Journal* 77 (1): 39–44.

Langer, Susanne K. 1957. *Philosophy in a New Key: A Study in the Symbolism of Reason, Rite, and Art.* 3d ed. Cambridge: Harvard University Press.

Rosenblatt, Louise M. 1976. *Literature as Exploration.* 3d ed. New York: Modern Language Association of America.

I The Collaborating and Creating Connection with Literature

1 Making Connections through Literature

Charles J. Nolan, Jr.
United States Naval Academy

When I first started teaching, almost twenty-five years ago now, something happened after class one day that startled me. The assignment had been *Lord of the Flies,* and after our first session on the novel, a student stayed behind to tell me of his reaction to the book. He had finished it late the night before, he noted, and had been so unnerved by Golding's work that he had thrown it violently to the floor. In my inexperience, I said something bland about the power of literature, but I did not see the situation as the opportunity to teach that it really was. I did not know then that the affective realm was the place to begin a discussion of powerful literature.

Since that time I have come to see that the "structure of feeling," to borrow a phrase from Raymond Williams (1966), that a work creates in us is, perhaps, the most important key to understanding and the reason why some books go so well in the classroom. I have also come to believe that a crucial part of any literature course is what happens *to* students as a result of both their confrontation with a text and our discussion of it.

The critical view that underlies my argument has its links to an earlier time and may seem outdated in these post-modern, post-structuralist days. One of the reasons, stated or not, that students come to college and to literature is to learn something about life. Even the most practical-minded, most vocationally oriented student knows that a course in literature has another dimension than the purely cerebral; and, in fact, many students enroll in our courses because their hunger for education has not been fully satisfied by other parts of the curriculum. So they are ready—even eager—to explore what the books we assign have to offer. Oh, they know they will have to learn something about how individual texts work, and they are willing to accept and master a certain amount of critical lingo, but the main show for them is that list of books.

The best place to begin, then, I believe, is with the emotional realm. Hence, my first question on a particular text is always directed not to the mind but to the feelings. "How did this book (or play or poem) make you feel?" I ask. This is a disturbing question for some students; they want to tell me instead what the book is about, but initially I will not let them. "Yes," I say, "your comments are perceptive. But how did the work make you *feel*?" Though some will give up in frustration—a particularly telling response—most will eventually shift to the emotional territory the text explores.

A few examples. One of the works I use in my contemporary American literature course to represent the racial climate of the sixties is *Soul on Ice.* With its provocative analysis of the connection between sexuality and racism, the book often stirs powerful emotions, emotions complicated by the natural reluctance to discuss those feelings in a racially mixed classroom. So when I ask my students how Cleaver's book makes them feel, I am prepared for initial silence. Usually, though, someone will hazard a relatively benign if open-ended comment, and, after a bit more sputtering, the discussion will take off. But several years ago, our first day on the book was a disappointment. In that particular class, there were only two black students, and one of them—a male athlete—was absent. As our discussion hovered around boredom, the other black class member sat staring at her notebook, and the white students seemed tentative or uncommunicative. Because it seemed as if my usual approach was not going to work, I moved on to questions of meaning and technique, and we stumbled through the rest of the hour.

In our next class, with both black students present, I continued where we had left off, examining Cleaver's literary devices. After a question or two, the athlete raised his hand and asked that dreamboat question for any English teacher. "I see some of what Cleaver is doing," he said. "But how is all this put together?" On any other day, I would have used the question for obvious purposes. But because I had been frustrated by what had happened the previous hour, I said, "Well, we covered some of that last time, but what *I'd* really like to know is how *you* responded to the book's subject matter." There was a momentary pause, and then that young black man spoke for five minutes straight. He told us about the uneasiness he felt on a largely white campus where most blacks were not students but kitchen help, about how he cringed when he saw another black with a big radio propped on his shoulder, about the pressure he felt to represent his race effectively among his classmates. And he told us about going on weekends to the local collegiate hangouts and dancing with white women, but never, *never,* asking for their phone numbers, even when he knew the chemistry was right. When he finished, other students, stunned by his honesty, began to tell tentatively of their attitudes and of their current struggles with the biases they had been raised with. It was one of the best classes I have ever had, though for the moment literary matters were forgotten.

Another case, this time in a freshman class studying *Cat on a Hot Tin Roof.* Because the issue of homosexuality is so central to Williams's characterization in the play, I look for ways to crystallize—at the emotional level—the crisis Brick faces. I tell the class about a friend of mine who recounts meeting his college roommate ten years after graduation and having the person he had lived with for four years confess his long-untold desires for my friend. When I finish, there is usually some expression of disgust by one or two class members, documenting anew the homophobic nature of American culture. But after class equilibrium has been regained, I ask my students, who attend a largely male and entirely residential school, how they would feel if that night after dinner their roommate made a similar confession. Another explosion, this time with one of the men blurting out, "That happened to me." He told of receiving a letter from his roommate of the previous year in which his friend declared his love for him.

"What did you do?" I asked.

"I tore the letter up," he said, "and didn't answer it!"

"How come?"

"I don't know."

We moved on then to other responses, as we worked through the various issues that were raised.

But the story doesn't end there. At the beginning of the next class, the same student raised his hand. "Why did I tear up the letter?" he asked. "Maybe your classmates can help," I responded, and then one after another they offered possible, though not very convincing, reasons for his action. When the discussion played out, we went on. But at the start of the next class, there he was again with his hand in the air. "Did we decide why I did that?" he wanted to know. It was at that moment that I could finally lead him and his classmates to a full understanding of just why Brick is so paralyzed by Skipper's admission.

What happens in class, however, is just the first step in helping students bring into focus what a particular text has meant to them—what values or beliefs it has reinforced or challenged, what difference it has made in their own lives. The next part of the process is to ask students to write about the books they have found energizing. Here I offer ample room. For those who find the emotional connection with literature threatening, I make some suggestions for standard analysis; but for others, who wish to explore further the highly charged issues the text and our discussion of it have raised, I provide the chance to work at the personal level. The first assignment in my contemporary American literature class, for example, makes the alternatives clear.

> For this paper, as for all your essays this semester, the topic is open. The only requirement is that your writing spring in some way from the literature we are reading. By the 17th, we will have read three long works—*The Crucible, Catch-22,* and *Cuckoo's Nest*—and several short stories and poems. Perhaps you would like to write an explication of some literary aspect of one of the works—the way Heller or Kesey use their titular metaphor for thematic purposes, for example, or the wisdom of dropping Act II, Scene 2, from Miller's play. Perhaps you would like to discuss the effectiveness of characterization in one of the stories or the use of imagery in one of the poems. Perhaps, on the other hand, you might prefer to use the literature we have read as a point of departure, linking your reading with your experience. How has the difficulty of maintaining relationships, described, for example, in Smiley's "Lily" or Edwards's "Roses," affected you, perhaps as children of divorced parents or as contemporary men and women seeking a future with another person? Do you find the craziness of life described in *Catch-22* or *Cuckoo's Nest* relevant to your own struggles in the contemporary world? Has the kind of hysteria Miller describes in *The Crucible* touched your life?
>
> Two kinds of essay, then, are possible: the strictly literary analysis or the use of literature as a springboard. Whatever you choose to write about, make it something that engages you at the most vital level. If you choose such a topic, your writing will sing. I'll look forward to reading your papers.

Typically, about a third of the students will choose to treat personal experience, though the percentage is often higher on subsequent assignments. And sometimes the essays are startling in their perceptiveness and power. A paper I received on *Native Son* from a white student in another course, for example, made me gasp. Near the end of an eight-page essay in which she documented her struggle with Wright's unsettling novel, she wrote:

> Although I wanted to cry, although I wanted to relieve myself from the burden of this book, I could not. I could not cry because I hated Bigger for being selfish and violent. I could not cry because I hated the Daltons for blinding themselves to the

> real causes of oppression. I could not cry because I hated Max for allowing eloquence to cloud his wisdom. I could not cry over Bigger, Mary, or Max because, in the end, I felt that they had received what they deserved. I could not cry because Bigger and I are products of our society, and our society does not cry for us. A cold statement, but *Native Son* is a cold novel. It is a book that destroys hope, ideals, even tears. The horror of *Native Son* is in the recognition of my racial pride and ultimately my racial prejudices.

Sometimes, however, the power of literature to affect values and behavior is not so immediately recognized; sometimes the change begun by a student's confrontation with a text reaches its culmination only later. A year after a course in Hemingway that I had taught at Johns Hopkins, I received a letter from one of the participants who told me how her reading had clarified some difficult feelings for her. When she had gone home for her father's funeral, she wrote, she found her mother and her six siblings in sharp disagreement. Her brothers and sisters and their spouses wanted an open casket; her mother wanted it closed but did not have the strength to hold out against her assembled children. To her youngest, my student, she explained that she wanted to remember her husband's smile and that seeing him as the mortician had prepared him just did not "*feel* right." Recounting what happened next, my correspondent wrote:

> I promised her that she would not have to see my father "that way," but hadn't a clue as to how I, the baby sister, could make a convincing argument for Mother's case, alone against the twelve of them.
>
> I'm writing this to tell you that as I entered the living room and stared down at those 12 upturned, closed-mouth faces, from out of nowhere, NOWHERE, came the memory of you reading aloud from *The Sun Also Rises* [the passage in which Jake defines immorality as that which makes us feel "disgusted afterwards"], and so I said it: "Mother says that seeing Daddy for the last time lying in a casket doesn't feel right. What's right is what feels right afterward; what's wrong is what feels wrong afterward. Mother will not be looking at Daddy." And she didn't.

I would argue that the powerful connections students make between their reading and their living are central to the study of literature, though I suspect that some of my colleagues would wonder about my approach. I can hear them say that what we have to offer students is a sophisticated understanding of the formal aspects of literature, and it is that particular body of knowledge that makes what we do different from what the psychologist, the sociologist, and the historian do. I would answer that what makes our discipline different from those others that treat human joys and sorrows is that literature makes us *feel* the plight of people caught up in a particular problem; literature puts us vicariously and emotionally in the situation the characters are struggling with, and therefore helps us to understand the author's vision of life in a way that a sociological or historical analysis of the issue can never do. It is precisely at the affective level that literature makes its most profound impact, and to refuse to discuss the emotional structure of books is to overlook part of what is distinctive about our subject.

"But what about the danger of what you're doing?" I hear my colleagues ask. "After all, you're not a therapist. What right have you to be fooling around with students' feelings?" A troubling question, I agree. Sometimes students are shaken by their confrontation with a text, in part as a result of our discussion of it, though mostly in the salutary way in which literature reorganizes our perspective of a particular issue. Occasionally, it is true, the impact that a book has had on a student has seemed to me excessive; and, where that has been the case, I have not hesitated to suggest that perhaps professional help is in order. In these instances, of course, the literature has merely been ancillary to the unresolved psychological problems the student is dealing with.

Of course, exploring the affective realm is not *all* of what we do; it is merely where we start. The bulk of class time is spent examining how writers achieve their purposes—how, that is, they use the various elements of their chosen genre to make us see through their eyes and perhaps accept their vision. That is the usual work of literature teachers the world over, and it is our special province within the curriculum. But it is not all we can do with the texts we have chosen. We can go beyond the usual and take the risk of engagement that is central to education. If we dare, we can help our students to clarify, *for themselves,* the values and attitudes they hold. When we ask them how a particular text makes them feel, we have begun the process of making connections that leads to what Forster ([1936] 1964) calls the "developed heart."

References

Forster, E. M. [1936] 1964. Notes on the English Character. In *Abinger Harvest.* New York: Harcourt Brace Jovanovich.

Williams, Raymond. 1966. *Modern Tragedy.* Stanford, Calif.: Stanford University Press.

2 Developing the Social Conscience through Literature

Peter Smagorinsky
University of Oklahoma

In "The Political Imagination of the Young Adolescent," Joseph Adelson (1972) describes the stages of ideological development during adolescence. In early adolescence, children have an outlook that is particular, personal, and tangible; their thought is locked in the present; they have a simplistic sense of human motivation; they have faith in authoritarianism; they cannot think abstractly; they lack an investment in social issues; their concept of society is rudimentary; and they can consider only a limited number of perspectives at once, perhaps even only their own.

By the end of high school, a teenager has begun to develop a "weak" ideology, which Adelson defines as the "presence of attitudes *roughly* consistent with each other, and *more or less* organized in reference to a more encompassing, though perhaps tacit, set of political principles" (1972, 120–21). Adelson distinguishes this from a "strong" ideology, formed (if at all) later in life, which is "a highly structured, hierarchically ordered, internally consistent body of general principles from which specific attitudes follow" (1972, 120). Towards the end of high school, students develop an ability to see abstraction and generality; they begin to grasp concepts central to ideology, such as liberty and rights; they develop a sociocentric perspective, able to see "the big picture"; they develop a time perspective, beginning to understand historical antecedents and gaining a sense of consequences and alternative outcomes; they begin to understand human complexity; they develop a relativistic outlook; they become more critical and pragmatic, and therefore less accepting of laws and authority; and they get a better sense of competing interests, and therefore of individual and minority rights.

Adelson's findings can have a profound impact on curriculum development. They suggest that in the early years of secondary school, students should study literature concerned with concepts that are concrete, personal, and particular, and then progress through high school to literature in which the social radius expands to include society as a whole. By the end of high school, students should read literature that involves the consideration and integration of a variety of viewpoints and requires students to project consequences and alternatives. Literature, therefore, can help students with their cognitive as well as their psychological development, the two often coming together in the formation of a personal ideology. A teacher can help students understand and order their attitudes by developing units of instruction based on ideological concerns relative to their stages of development (Smagorinsky and Gevinson 1989).

Many schools require the study of American literature during the junior year. This is a propitious placement of "classic" American literature, which often involves themes central to ideological formation and comes at a time when most students are ready for it. Even literature that is difficult (i.e., Thoreau's "Civil Disobedience" and Emerson's "Self-Reliance"), if taught in the proper context and if directed toward students' own concerns and experiences, can be fruitful reading for average-ability students.

A variety of appropriate themes concerning a social ideology are possible in the American literature program. Students can study the individual and society, reading Emerson's "Self- Reliance," Thoreau's "Walden," and poetry by Frost and Dickinson. The theme of progress is explored by Thomas Berger in *Little Big Man,* by Faulkner in the stories of *Go Down, Moses,* by science fiction writers including Ursula Le Guin in *The Word for World Is Forest,* and by N. Scott Momaday in *The Way to Rainy Mountain.* Justice is at the heart of Melville's *Billy Budd,* Richard Wright's *Native Son,* Dee Brown's *Creek Mary's Blood,* and Toni Cade Bambara's *The Salt Eaters.*

An excellent unit for high school juniors to study is the American tradition of protest. Students at this age, as Adelson notes, are losing their faith in authority and institutions and are beginning to develop their own sense of what is right. As we know from our experiences with teenagers (and adults), often this perspective is narrow, focusing on their own particular concerns, *right* being defined as what best serves their own interests. Yet students at this age are capable of forming a more sociocentric perspective, which in turn allows them to consider the rights of others. They are also beginning to have an investment in social issues. Protest literature helps students understand the relative fairness of human action, and how the behavior of majorities and authority figures affects the rights of others. Thinkers such as Thoreau and Martin Luther King, Jr., who articulate the role of conscience in social behavior, force us to consider that we have a moral responsibility to protest what we think is wrong. For students who feel the oppression of rules and restrictions, who have the feeling that something is wrong and imbalanced in the world but do not have channels of response, reading such literature is a means for ordering their thoughts and understanding potentials and possibilities for action.

Prior to reading, students could do an activity that prepares them for the concepts in the literature. For instance, they could clip newspaper or magazine articles that relate accounts of apartheid protests, union strikes, acts of terrorism, student rebellion, and so on for class discussion. What are the conditions prompting the protest? What types of action are appropriate? *Why* are they appropriate? Is there a series of steps we can take in protesting unfair treatment? Can we use this sequence of steps consistently, regardless of the source and degree of oppression we face? Is violence ever justified in protesting? Consideration of these questions will help students explore the problems they will face later in the literature, and improve their comprehension of the issues.

Materials for this unit are available in many texts. For a historical precedent, students could study Patrick Henry's "Speech before the Virginia Convention" or other colonial rhetoric. The civil rights movement of the 1960s offers many literary protests, the most eloquent by Martin Luther King, Jr. Although his "I Have a Dream" speech is the most widely printed of King's works, his "Letter from a Birmingham Jail" is a more articulate statement of his nonviolent philosophy. Supplementary material could come from the excellent PBS documentaries "Eyes on the Prize" and "Martin Luther King: From Memphis to Montgomery." One point about using King: Because he has been canonized, modern students believe him and his nonviolent ethic to be the essence of the civil rights movement. He was, however, one of many leaders, a number of whom disagreed with his nonviolent approach. To give an accurate perspective on the civil rights movement, a teacher might want to include an essay by Huey Newton, Angela Davis, or other radical figures; the "Eyes on the Prize II" series offers compelling footage of Stokely Carmichael, Malcolm X, and others who advocated a more aggressive approach to social change than did King.

King's ideas are to a great extent predicated on Thoreau's "Civil Disobedience." Students might need more help in comprehending this difficult text, but it is essential reading in developing a political conscience. Other essays could come from the women's suffrage movement (Susan B. Anthony, Carrie Chapman Catt), or from the Equal Rights Amendment movement, both of which have filled anthologies with excellent protest writing. Another widely printed protest piece is Chief Joseph's "Nez Perce Surrender," an eloquent plea for dignity and acceptance for Native Americans following their defeat.

Of all the literature I have used in this unit, the piece with the greatest impact has been Ken Kesey's *One Flew Over the Cuckoo's Nest.* I have used both the novel and the film, and each affects students profoundly. MacMurphy, who represents the trickster archetype and therefore appeals to the adolescent sense of rebellion, moves from being a self-centered mutineer to a conscience-guided social reformer. Many of my students have named this novel as the most relevant literary experience of their lives. The preparation they receive in studying the other writers is certainly responsible for their ability to place MacMurphy, the Big Nurse, and the inmates of the asylum in a philosophical perspective.

Student response to the issues could come through a variety of avenues. Possibilities include:

1. Students could keep a reading log in response to the literature and films, perhaps using their ideas to generate discussion questions and to determine topics for formal writing.
2. Students could role-play discussions of local issues; i.e., students could assume the roles of Martin Luther King, R. P. MacMurphy, Susan B. Anthony, Patrick Henry, and Stokely Carmichael to discuss solutions to such problems as local skateboard restrictions, oppressive school policies, and so on.
3. Students could write a formal expository essay delineating the conditions that must exist in order to justify various degrees of protest. In such a paper they might rank different types of protest from least severe to most severe and give examples from literature, history, or personal knowledge of when each stage is appropriate. Such an essay could help students internalize ideas from the unit and give them a course of action to take should they perceive a need to protest a situation.
4. Students could write an original protest in one of several forms: satire, letter to an offending party, letter to a media agency, dramatic script (perhaps performed or videotaped), or other mode of expression. Here, students are crossing the bridge between the abstract world of philosophy and the real world

of events, forcing them to bring their academic thinking in contact with their society. They are developing what Sandra Stotsky (1989) calls a "civic identity": "the psychological foundation for participation in the political process as a 'citizen,' as someone with a sense of the common good as well as a sense of one's own interests." Stotsky points out that civic education has been confined to social studies programs, but should be equally the province of literature study.

5. Students could lead discussions on the relative advantages and disadvantages of contrasting approaches to protest. For instance, after viewing the first three segments of the "Eyes on the Prize II" series, students could examine the pros and cons of the approaches taken by Martin Luther King, Stokely Carmichael (or other Black Panthers), and Malcolm X in fighting bigotry.
6. Students could research a historic protest movement, writing a paper analyzing the effectiveness of the methods of protest in light of the conditions prompting it and perhaps presenting the research to the class.
7. Students could perform oral interpretations of poetry such as Langston Hughes's "Ballad of the Landlord," Lance Jeffers's "On Listening to the Spirituals," Paul Laurence Dunbar's "Sympathy," Dudley Randall's "The Idiot," Claude McKay's "The White House," Countée Cullen's "Any Human to Another," and Arna Bontemps's "A Black Man Talks of Reaping."
8. Students could create art—including a collage, sculpture, painting, and so on—that expresses or illustrates a protest.
9. Students could retell a scene from *One Flew Over the Cuckoo's Nest* from two perspectives, the Nurse's and MacMurphy's.

A unit of this type helps students connect with literature in an important way. I often get students who start to protest unfair rules at home and in school, at times starting petitions to protest a rule or policy. Occasionally I get a student like Dorothy, who wrote me these (unedited) remarks on her semester evaluation.

> As you know I am moving and because of this class is one of the reasons why.
>
> We really got into alot of heavy discussions in this class about some deep issues. I, for one, was effected greatly. When we began talking about "protest" and standing up for what you believe in. I would get angry and confused not just in class but at home, my parents noticed it and my friends, but mostly I did. You see, Ive never been one to fight back, or try and get

> my way. If their was any compromising to be done in a situation, though it may effect me in a wrong way, *I* usually did it. And it didn't bother me. (At least I thought it didn't.)
>
> As we talked more in class and I learned more, I began to protest more and more (even about little things). The strange thing is I wasn't doing it purposely. I didn't realize it at all. Not until later on, anyway.
>
> I wasnt protesting in a bad way I just wasn't compromising myself anymore. Although others didn't see it that way, but if I was looking through their eyes at me I don't think I'd see it my way either.
>
> It seems that I have aquired a whole new set of values. I feel very strongly about them and also that they are good. In order to live according to these values, I felt it necessary to make a few drastic changes in my life, which I am in the process of doing.
>
> I wish I could be more specific in what I mean but in order to do that I would have to tell you my whole life story. I wish I could tell you, I think you would find it interesting.

I later found out that she had been living with relatives at the convenience of others, and had decided to move in with an aunt in a different part of the country and live according to what she felt was best for *her*.

Of course, Dorothy's response was extraordinary, hardly representative of how most kids react. But most students reveal in their evaluations a greater commitment to following their conscience, often citing specific examples of ways in which they've stood up for what they think is right.

A unit of this type helps students connect with literature in an important way. I have taught this unit for several years now, and feel personally renewed and more socially responsible each time I teach it. It is hard to be indifferent to the world's wrongs when they go against your conscience; as Thoreau says, to do so is to be no better than a lump of dirt.

References

Adelson, Joseph. 1972. The Political Imagination of the Young Adolescent. In *Twelve to Sixteen: Early Adolescence,* edited by Jerome Kagan and Robert Coles, 106–43. New York: W. W. Norton.

Smagorinsky, Peter, and Steven Gevinson. 1989. *Fostering the Reader's Response: Rethinking the Secondary Literature Curriculum.* Palo Alto, Calif.: Dale Seymour Publications.

Stotsky, Sandra. 1989. Literature Programs and the Development of Civic Identity. *The Leaflet* 88 (1): 17–21.

3 Connecting with Literature: Activities for *The Cay* and *The Bedspread*

Vicki L. Olson
Augsburg College

"Sh-h-h, she's going to read now!" The children settle themselves, an elusive calmness envelops the room, and the story begins. Teachers and students who share books regularly recognize this pleasurable pattern and understand its positive effects on their classrooms. The enjoyment garnered from storytime is enough to justify its presence in the daily schedule, and often that is precisely its best purpose. But there are special books that lead so easily and smoothly to writing, thinking, and creating that not to take advantage of them is a wasted opportunity.

In this chapter, I offer activities and ideas to use in conjunction with two books that I think are special: *The Cay* by Theodore Taylor (1969, Doubleday) and *The Bedspread* by Sylvia Fair (1982, William Morrow).

The activities for the picture book, *The Bedspread,* are designed to appeal to students of different learning styles. Discussions during and after the activities can help students think about themselves as learners, as well as extend their enjoyment of the book. Special books generate special and varied responses. Allowing children to choose their form of response can increase its depth and their personal involvement. This lesson offers a range of activities for students, who can choose the option that appeals to them the most.

Activities for *The Cay* are designed to be used in response to selected chapters of the book. Students can keep their responses in a simple construction-paper folder, thus creating their own response journals. This kind of activity could be duplicated with most any book that individual teachers deem special. It takes rereading and some thought to pinpoint appropriate types of responses for each chapter, but beyond that the task is not difficult.

Writing in response to literature allows for a different, more reflective response than listening. Writing often causes students to synthesize and analyze more than they would if they just listened. Discussing responses at a later point can further the use of these critical thinking skills. Writing a response ahead of time may also encourage more individual involvement in the discussion; i.e., if students' thoughts are already formulated, it is easier to share them. In this situation, you are not so much teaching writing as using writing as a tool to aid thinking.

You will need to decide how often to ask students to write. Questions and suggestions are provided for most chapters, but they need not all be used. Select what interests you and fits your time frame. You will also need to structure the follow-up discussion/sharing sessions. These are very important and should be used to prevent this from becoming just another "read and answer questions" exercise.

Response may sometimes combine writing and drawing. Be sure to include the drawing, too, in the sharing sessions.

The Cay by Theodore Taylor

Chapter 1. Phillip said he had heard a lot about war, but never seen one. List three or four things that you think could happen to Phillip and his family now that the Germans have attacked Aruba and brought war to "the warm, blue Caribbean." Remember that Phillip is one of the main characters in this book so he probably would not be killed.

Before starting Chapter 2, have students report the various possibilities they have listed. You could write them on chart paper and save them to see if any of the students' ideas match what actually happens in the book.

Chapter 2. Use a large map or globe to show students where Curaçao is and how they might travel to get to Miami and then to Curaçao. Ask students to write their prediction for whether or not Phillip and his mother will make it to Miami, and why or why not.

Allow three to five minutes for students to think and write. Then put students in groups of three to five and have them share their predictions and reasons. Ask each group to develop a group prediction and reason. This prediction/reason might be the same as one of the group member's or it might be made up of portions of several members' individual predictions/reasons. Have each group share its group prediction and reasoning.

Chapter 3. Sketch what you think Timothy and Phillip's raft looked like. Remember to include as many details about it as you can recall. Label the things you put on the raft.

Share sketches with partners. Help each other develop detailed sketches.

List two or three words or phrases that you think describe Timothy. Tell why.

Talk briefly about a few of their lists. Encourage students to explain their choices.

Chapter 6. Timothy and Phillip have been on the raft several days. Phillip is blind. Only one airplane has been heard in all their time at sea. The island Timothy spots is small, uninhabited, and without fresh water. He decides they will land on the island rather than continue on the raft. Do you agree or disagree with Timothy's decision? Give reasons to explain your thoughts.

Discuss students' answers. Make a chart titled "Pros and Cons for Landing" and another one titled "Pros and Cons for Continuing on the Raft." As students explain their reasons, write them in the appropriate columns on the charts. Add any other pros and cons they think of but have not written down. As a group, consider the list of pros and cons and decide as a group whether Timothy's decision was a wise one.

Chapter 7. Sketch what you imagine the island looks like. You might do two views: a side view like you would have just sailing towards it, and a top view like you would have flying over it. Include as many of the things Timothy said were on the island as you can recall.

Share sketches in groups of three to five students. Then in these same groups, have students make two lists, which will be used in a large-group discussion:

> Things on the island that will help them survive.
>
> Things not on the island that they still will need to survive.

As a large group, share each group's second list. Write the items down. Then discuss what Timothy should do first to ensure survival and why. Try to come to a whole-group decision.

Chapter 8. Timothy could not read or write enough to spell the word *help.* If you had to describe Timothy, would you say he was intelligent? Why or why not?

Discuss responses briefly as a whole group.

Chapter 9. Phillip said he had begun to change. What are some ways that you see Phillip changing from the boy who first woke up on the raft with Timothy and Stew Cat?

Discuss responses. List the ways Phillip has changed. Discuss why.

Chapter 11. Timothy and Phillip are in a dangerous situation—living on an uninhabited island that no one seems to pass by, fly over, or know about. Yet even in this situation, they've had good luck, too. With a partner, brainstorm two lists: a "good luck" list and a "bad luck" list. Think of the things that seem to have worked in Timothy and Phillip's favor and the things that seem to work against them.

As a whole group, discuss the lists. Then, brainstorm the kinds of things that might cause Phillip to say, "But [our luck] didn't change. It got worse." Have students predict what might happen next, given the present situation.

Chapter 12. Malaria is a disease that people who live in the tropics can get. Write what you know (or think you know) about it. Read about malaria in a dictionary. Add to and/or change what you first wrote about malaria.

As a group, define malaria. Then discuss how Timothy might have contracted it; how he knew he had it; and what might happen because he had it again.

Chapter 13. Why would Phillip ask, "Timothy, are you still black?" Write your thoughts.

Give students a few minutes to think and write. Then discuss their ideas.

Chapter 16. List as many changes as you can that Phillip learned from Timothy that will help him to survive. Do you think Phillip would have as strong a chance at survival had he landed in the same situation with his father rather than with Timothy? Explain your answer.

Compile a group list of the things Phillip learned from Timothy. Discuss.

Also discuss how people can be intelligent in very different ways; i.e., Phillip learned about geography from books; Timothy learned about hurricanes by living through them. Whose "intelligence" would be valued the most in our world today? Why?

Chapter 19. Phillip returned to Curaçao a very different person. What are some ways he has changed?

Discuss.

Memorials are sometimes built or created to honor the dead. What might be a fitting memorial for Timothy? How might Phillip pay tribute to the man who taught him to survive?

Discuss, design, and share.

***The Bedspread* by Sylvia Fair†**

1. Share *The Bedspread* with the students. Be sure to share the pictures, too.
2. As a group, discuss the book:
   - Focus on the sisters. Have students tell about the characteristics of Amelia and Maud. List these in two columns on a large sheet of paper. Students will need to use the book's pictures as well as the text to infer what the sisters were like.
   - Focus on the bedspread. Ask students to recall some of the things the sisters sewed on the bedspread. Have them describe the differences in the ways the sisters remembered and created their home. You might list the items as students describe them.
   - Do a quick "whip" around the circle. Ask each student to briefly tell which part of the bedspread she or he liked best and why. Have them also tell which sister's version of the item they liked best; i.e., Amelia's garden or Maud's door. You might covertly tally which sister is mentioned most often. Afterwards, report to students which sister they chose most often as a group. Have them speculate on why so many of them chose work done by that sister.
3. Choose individual writing activities. It may take students two or three days to complete the activity of their choice. You might want to make a handout that describes each option so students have a written reference. If necessary, adapt the wording to fit your students.

   A. Ask three people the same five to seven questions. Write down their answers. Also, answer the questions yourself. Find out who is most like you and most different from you. Make a chart that shows what you learned (Figure 1).

† Portions of the lesson written by Vicki L. Olson for *The Bedspread* appear in *Learning and Teaching Style: In Theory and Practice,* 1988, Columbia, Conn.: The Learner's Dimension. Reprinted and adapted by permission of the copyright holder, Kathleen A. Butler.

Name	Q1	Q2	Q3	Q4	Q5
Me					
Joe					
Mom	(answers to questions go in this space)				
Anne					

__________ is most like me because:

__________ is most different from me because:

Sample questions: What's your favorite ice cream flavor? If you could be an animal, what would you be? Why? Plus any other questions you want to ask.

Figure 1. Chart for students to complete

B. Think of a place that is special to you. Create a collage that shows this place and how it makes you feel. Use pictures from magazines, scraps of fabric and paper, markers, and whatever else you wish to make your collage. Then write about the place you are showing in your collage and your feelings about this place.

C. Design and draw your own bedspread that shows important parts of your home (or one you used to live in). Remember that Amelia and Maud showed both the house and the yard. And when they couldn't remember something exactly, they made things up a little. Choose the sister you like the most—Amelia or Maud—and write her a letter. Tell her about the home you showed in your bedspread design and how you showed your feelings about it.

D. Ask an adult you know (parent, relative, friend) to tell you about memories of a home from his or her childhood. Work with that person to draw the house, yard, garden, and whatever else he or she recalls. Save this drawing and include it with your report.

Write a short report on what the adult told you. Describe the picture you drew together. Tell about what your person liked and didn't like about this home. Maybe your person told you a funny or interesting story about something that happened there. You could include that in your report, too.

4. When the individual activities are completed, provide a sharing time where students can show and tell about what they did.

This could be done as a whole group or in a smaller, cooperative group setting. Then display the options—drawings, collages, and writing.

5. After activities have been shared, discuss with the children the choices they made.
   - Why did they choose the option they did? What made it appealing to them?
   - Were they glad they chose that option? Or does a different option now seem more appealing? Why?
   - When you have choices to make about work activities, what things can help you select the best option for you?

4 Using Journals and Small Groups to Explore Literature

JoAnna Stephens Mink
Mankato State University

A few semesters ago, after a rather dismal experience with teaching a college-level, required, freshman second-semester course that combined composition and literature, I decided to alter radically my approach, to move toward what theorists have termed a student-centered classroom. I didn't change the number of writing assignments; I didn't change the reading list; I didn't change my grading standards or expectations. The only two changes I made were to assign a journal and to implement small-group discussions. The result was one of my most rewarding teaching experiences. Students wrote daily about literature; they talked and argued about literature; they even acted out literary texts. I had stumbled upon an approach that met my students' needs in helping them become engaged in their own learning.

It is a commonplace that reading and writing involve the same kinds of acts: In order to write well, one must also be able to read well, to identify the cues and the techniques that make an essay, a piece of fiction, a poem "work." Whether we are engaged in reading or in writing, the function of language remains constant—to make meaning. Joseph Comprone, for example, says that when we combine these activities, "reading is as much an act of composing as writing" (1983). Likewise, David Bleich supports the interrelationship between reading and responding in *Readings and Feelings: An Introduction to Subjective Criticism* (1975). The response journal has become an important part of many curricula, as educators at all levels have become convinced of its importance in bridging the gap between the parts of the communication triangle (Emig 1977; Fulwiler 1980; Petersen 1982). We must, however, continue to seek assignments and teaching methods that will involve our students in as many ways as possible with the material. In courses that involve literature, this multidimensional approach is particularly important in order to encourage response and growth on the part of our students.

I use the same basic assignment for all my courses that include literature. In addition to reading the works, students must write a journal entry about each work before class discussion. Their entries, about 200 words in length or fifteen minutes of focused writing, should demonstrate their exploration of an aspect of the work that they find intriguing or confusing or interesting. I encourage them to explore the work in relation to themselves, to do what I call "making the literature part of themselves." Class time is usually lively, because they all have something to add to our discussion since they already have thought and written about the work. After each class discussion, students then must write another entry of about 250 words in which they continue to explore their previous line of thinking, or in which they react to something said in class. For example, they now may have a better understanding of the literary text and they can react in a more focused way. Or they may disagree with something said in class, either by a classmate or by me.

Since most students have not kept a literary response journal before, they usually need some guidance as to how to begin. On the first day of the semester, I use Kate Chopin's "The Story of an Hour" to illustrate one way they may use their journal to respond to the text.† Since they cannot have prepared for this first class meeting, they all approach the work on a more or less equal footing. First, they read silently the first half of the story (finishing with the paragraph that begins "Now her bosom rose and fell tumultuously"). They then write for five to ten minutes about what they think the story is about and how they think it will end, paying particular attention to clues that Chopin plants in her description of Mrs. Mallard and of the spring day. We discuss the reasons for their conjectures. Then, students read the rest of the story down to the paragraph beginning "Someone was opening the front door with a latchkey." (I have them put a piece of paper over the last three paragraphs so they won't be tempted to continue reading.) They again write about their impression of this second section—whether their original conjectures have been accurate and how they think the story will end. We discuss these, and then they read the last three paragraphs and discuss the entire story. This assignment achieves three important purposes: Students respond immediately and in writing to the text; they discuss their opinions about the text; and

† I am indebted to former colleague Janet Doubler Ward for suggesting this assignment.

they learn something about techniques of fiction writing. This type of introduction not only gets the semester off to a good start, but it also presents the journal as a nonthreatening place for them to record their feelings and opinions about a literary text.

Writing Prompts Are Helpful

At the beginning of the semester, I suggest writing prompts that students may respond to in their journals. After four or five weeks, they are usually fairly adept at writing journal entries, so I do not provide the prompts unless they ask for them or unless I conclude from reading their first set of entries (I collect the journals every four weeks) that they need further guidance. Examples of these prompts include the following:

- "Young Goodman Brown"—(1) Explore the relationship between people presented in the story, especially between Brown and his wife. (2) What do you think is "our nature and our destiny" according to Hawthorne? (3) Does it really matter whether or not Brown dreamed his experience? (4) Compare the theme of "Young Goodman Brown" to that of one of the other stories we have read.
- "The Secret Sharer"—(1) Trace and discuss the relationship between the captain and Leggatt. (2) Who is the secret sharer? What is the reader's relationship to this story? (3) Have you ever experienced a bifurcation of your nature? Describe and tell how you resolved it.
- "Hansel and Gretel"—(1) Tell who (either Hansel or Gretel) solved each of the problems presented in the fairy tale. (2) Write a story with a contemporary setting that presents the same theme. (3) Find an important symbol in the story (e.g., the birds) and tell how it is significant.

These writing prompts and before-class journal entries achieve several goals: Students are not reading passively; they must focus on one or two important aspects of the literature. They come to class armed with something to say about the work, ideas to test against the responses of their peers. Writing journal entries is a comparatively unstressful way of discussing the literature; because they focus on their own personal explorations of the work, students have the opportunity to explore before they must write their formal paper assignments. Finally, when it comes time to select a paper topic, they can refer to their journals for some "germs" that they can develop.

As the semester progresses, students' entries become more focused as they begin to see the journal as a valuable tool for understanding the works. The following journal entries, written by a fairly average student about F. Scott Fitzgerald's "Babylon Revisited," illustrate some aspects of what I try to get my students to do in their journals. The "before" entry begins with and focuses on the identification of an issue. The student concludes the entry by enlarging upon the theme, with the idea that the situation described in the story is a general one and not limited to the story's characters. The "after" entry begins by responding to something said in class discussion and then takes the idea further. In both of these unedited entries we see the student's engagement with the text in phrases such as "The impression I get" and "I think" and "I admire."

> *Before-class entry:* The issue I want to talk about in this journal entry is whether or not Charlie will ever get back Honoria again. The impression I get is that he will not. The main reason is because of Marion. As long as she is still living he will never get her back. Marion is too jealous of Charlie because he made all that money without working. She and Lincoln worked hard and still did not make much to spend on "wants" but instead had to spend on "needs." She also has resentment towards Charlie because she puts all the blame on him for her sister Helen dieing. Honoria is the one thing that Charlie needs and wants. Marion sees that Charlie suffers without Honoria. This is Marion's way of getting back at Charlie. Marion can't forgive Charlie for his past even though she sees that he has changed. I feel sorry for Charlie and Honoria because they both want to be with each other but one woman's inability to forgive ruins a potential relationship between a father and his daughter.

> *After-class entry:* In the class discussion on "Babylon Revisited" we came to the conclusion that the point Fitzgerald was trying to make is that what one does in the past cannot be erased. I figured our the meaning of the story while I read it the night before. I think everyone knows that Fitzgerald's point is true. In Charlie's case Marion has not forgotten about his past but neither has Charlie. I admire Charlie because he admitted he was wrong and by doing this he changed. He has proven this and Marion knows that but her jealousy and hatred toward him keeps him and Honoria apart. I think she truly cares about the little girl but I think her own self interests dominate over what is right. If people admit that they were wrong and they do something to change, then they need to be evaluated in a fair way. The past is the past. It's over and done with.

I was delighted that the student even compliments himself for identifying the theme; this to me indicates he is becoming more confident about his reading. This student has demonstrated his exploration of the work from a personal viewpoint, shows some honest response to the text, and has made it part of himself.

Small Groups Encourage Full Participation

By exploring literary texts in journal entries, students better understand the works and write more effectively about them. To reinforce this personal and generally nonguided exploration, I also make use of small-group discussions during class, and I think that to be effective, these two methods must be used jointly. I decided to use small groups to encourage my students to become actively involved in the discussion of the literature. Discussions in groups of five or six students force them to become active participants in the learning process (and part of their course grade is based on class participation). The focus of the class then shifts from the instructor to the students seated in circles helping each other make sense of the text.

When we resume our "traditional" seating arrangement, my role is that of moderator. I ask a question relating to one of their small-group "tasks," and the discussion is on. Encouraging students to participate in class discussion is no longer a problem, because they have already discussed their ideas with their peers in the more comfortable small-group situation. Since I began using this method of class discussion, I have found that we seem to cover the works as thoroughly as when I provided most of the information. It usually takes a bit longer to get to the point where I feel we have discussed the important aspects of the works, so my classes tend to focus on depth rather than breadth.

I have used this method successfully even in my large survey classes because students, by becoming engaged in interpreting the text, learn valuable skills that help them interpret the works by themselves. In other words, they are learning the skills of literary interpretation and communication of their ideas, certainly a more important goal than merely memorizing particular facts about a specific work. In addition, they find that they enjoy reading and discussing literature. Often their after-class journal entries focus on something said in their small group, which somehow was not brought up in class, indicating to me that they are learning about the reading and writing experience.

At the end of my first semester of using the journal assignment, I asked my second-semester freshmen to evaluate their experiences. The following comments are representative:

> I like the journal. The more I write in it, the more confident I get about my own writing. Since we don't have to worry about spelling and punctuation, we can focus more on just writing our ideas.
>
> Sometimes after reading a particular story or poem I am puzzled at its meaning. I then start to write in my journal and I can see the progress that I am making to understand the work.
>
> I must admit that in the beginning I thought the journal was just too much extra work for me to do. However, I realize that by writing freestyle my thoughts and ideas about a particular article of literature is very helpful when I sat down to write my paper.

This last example sums up exactly what I had hoped the students would learn through this experience:

> I really enjoy writing in my journal because it helps me to understand the literature better. I write how I feel about the story before the class as a whole discusses it. Writing in my journal also prepares me for small group discussion. Without my journal, I would be lost.

Of course, using this method necessitates some changes, not only in class format but also in our thinking about our roles as teachers. Explaining the assignment and my expectations for the journal takes some class time, but I have found that I spend a total of perhaps two or three hours during the whole semester discussing journal writing. The advantages of this method overwhelmingly outweigh any extra time spent. An observer of my classes would not see students taking copious notes or hanging on to my every word. Instead, they would see students actively engaged in their own learning, sometimes even arguing rather heatedly, but this, I think, is positive because the students clearly are engaged in the discussion.

The most important advantage is reflected in the students' comments I have quoted. By using this method, we merge various skills of communication: (1) independent reading and thinking and writing about ideas presented in literature, (2) sharing of those ideas in small or large groups, (3) the chance to reevaluate those ideas in the entries written after class discussion, and (4) the articulation of ideas in formal writing assignments, either as papers or examinations. This synthesis is exciting for me as an instructor, as I see even normally silent students become engaged in communicating their ideas to others, and I believe it is exciting for the students as well.

References

Bleich, David. 1975. *Readings and Feelings: An Introduction to Subjective Criticism.* Urbana, Ill.: National Council of Teachers of English.

Comprone, Joseph. 1983. Recent Research in Reading and Its Implications for the College Composition Curriculum. *Rhetoric Review* 1: 122–37.

Emig, Janet. 1977. Writing as a Mode of Learning. *College Composition and Communication* 28: 122–28.

Fulwiler, Toby. 1980. Journals across the Disciplines. *English Journal* 69: 14–19.

Petersen, Bruce T. 1982. Writing about Responses: A Unified Model of Reading, Interpretation, and Composition. *College English* 44: 459–68.

5 Poetry to Engage the Person

Nancy Gorrell
Morristown High School
Morristown, New Jersey

When I first began teaching high school English in the early 1970s, I engaged in a rather short-lived fantasy. My passion was poetry, and I dreamed of sharing my favorite poems with excited and receptive students. We would discuss poetry, inspire each other, and write poems together. I would sit with my students in a sharing circle (credits to Ken Macrorie and the student-centered classroom), reading passages from T. S. Eliot's "The Love Song of J. Alfred Prufrock" while the boys' chests swelled and the girls all sighed. The reality? Silence—that dreadful silence in the classroom when we know we are talking more to ourselves than to anyone else. Why was it so difficult to talk about poems? Students I knew capable of animated discussions of music, film, and literature seemed tongue-tied when responding to poetry. They might be able to express "I liked it" or "I didn't like it," but they were rarely able to explain how or why.

Wedded to the view that the special meaning of poetry centered on its evocative and experiential nature as well as the nature of the reader's response, I knew I wanted my students to experience poetry, to empathize, to participate in the meaning-making of the poem, and thus, to ultimately appreciate poetry in its fullest sense. Too frequently I had heard moans and groans at the mention of poetry, and I was no longer willing to spend fruitless hours searching for poems to inspire my students, only to find myself the single appreciative respondent. But how could I begin to teach poetic appreciation?

The answer to my dilemma was certainly in a reader-response, aesthetic approach to poetry which would place the student in control of what was read, how poems were interpreted, discussed, and shared.[1] My goal was the integration of the total process of appreciative response: reading, interpreting (creating meaning), discussing, sharing, and writing. Although I had the approach, practical questions still remained. How to begin in the classroom?

The following five-lesson poetry unit has succeeded with my high school students for well over a decade. Its universal appeal makes it an ideal strategy for students of all ability levels. This plan requires no special materials except what is available in most English departments. Students engage in all learning activities:

Reading—researching and reading poetry

Writing—critical papers and original poetry

Speaking—small-group discussions, panel presentations, oral interpretations of poetry, large-group discussions

Listening—for understanding, to challenge presentations

Predicated on the empowered student, this strategy builds the values essential for appreciative learning: tolerance, respect, and understanding. In four weeks, we develop a sense of communal excitement, understanding, and appreciation of poetry which I can only describe as the joy of teaching.

Lesson One: Poetry Awareness Poll (One Day)

To set the stage for attitudinal change, I suggest to my students that we explore our poetic awareness. I distribute blank paper, and I ask for brief responses to these dictated questions:

1. Name five living, twentieth-century American poets.
2. Name five dead, twentieth-century American poets.
3. Recall one poem you liked. Name it. Can you remember lines from the poem? If so, write them down.
4. Have you ever written a poem for yourself—not assigned in school?
5. Have you ever shared a poem with another person—showed them a poem you liked, discussed it together?
6. Have you ever heard a poet read poetry in a live performance?
7. If you wanted to hear poets reading their poetry, would you know where to go to hear such performances?
8. Have you ever given a poem as a present to someone? You may or may not have written it yourself.
9. Do you have a favorite poet, excluding rock musicians? Name the poet.

10. Do you have a favorite poet/musician? Name the poet.
11. How do you feel about poetry? Comment.
12. What do you think poetry is? Comment.

These thought-provoking questions surprise and amuse the students. Most have never thought of poetry as performance or poetry as gifts. None of the students can name more than five American poets, dead or alive. Poets named are those taught frequently in school (e.g., Robert Frost, E. E. Cummings, Langston Hughes). Few students have favorite poets or memories of poems. Most think of poetry in an academic rather than experiential way. No one has ever attended a poetry reading. The poll is not only successful in exposing the students' limited experience and knowledge, it begins the attitude shift essential for appreciation. Students leave class curious about poetry, more open to its possibility, and with an emerging sense that "this just might be fun."

Lesson Two: Independent Reading Assignment (One Week)

On the second day, I distribute to each student the poetry textbooks for American literature available in my English department (*Poems: American Themes* and *20th Century America in Poetry: Landscapes of the Mind*). Any anthology is suitable as long as all students have the same materials. I tell the class that our aesthetic approach to poetry will require their active participation. They will be choosing the poems to read, discuss, and interpret. And what poems will they be? I tell the class that I want them to choose great poems—poems that excite, provoke, and inspire them. I stress that what is important is *their* understanding and appreciation of the poems and their ability to share this experience with others in the class.

I distribute the following assignment, telling the students to complete their reading in one week.

Independent Reading Assignment

Directions: Browse through your poetry textbook to select, in your opinion:

1. The most *beautiful* poem
2. The most *shocking* poem
3. The most *emotive* poem—it must cause your heart to "skip a beat"
4. The most *thought-provoking* poem
5. The most __________ poem (you choose the category—e.g., the most humorous, puzzling, romantic poems)

Read selectively, with interest and enthusiasm. Be sure to choose poems you understand and appreciate. Browse through the *entire* book before you make your final decisions. When you have chosen a poem for each category, write the title and page number for each poem on a separate piece of paper. Include a brief paragraph explaining your choice. Bring this paper and your book to class in one week.

Caution: Do not confer with other students in class when making your choices. These selections are to be your independent decisions.

Lesson Three: Small-Group Sharing, Discussing, and Interpreting (2–3 Days)

In an effort to compare and share the results of our independent search, I tell the students to choose one category of poems they would like to explore further. I list the categories (shocking, beautiful, etc.) on the board, selecting by show of hands volunteers for each. By this time, many students have developed preferences based on the poems they have found, and they react enthusiastically. I encourage the class to suggest the optional category, and often the students choose humor. I divide the typical class of twenty-five students into five groups of five students each.

Once in groups, students are eager to share results. They are curious to see the poems others have selected, and they are surprised when choices are similar (this frequently occurs). I explain that each group of students must debate among themselves in order to select the *one* exemplary poem within their category to present to the class as a whole. I stress that each group must share at least five poems (one offered by each group member) before reaching a consensus. To facilitate the selection process, I distribute to each group this task worksheet.

Small-Group Instructions

1. Determine/define the nature of your category.
   a. What is shock? How does it affect you? What emotional reactions does it cause?
   b. What is beauty? Is it just "in the eyes of the beholder"? What makes a beautiful poem? Beautiful words, images, etc.? What is beauty to you?
   c. What does emotive mean? Can a poem cause your heart to skip a beat? Select the poem that evokes many different emotional responses (not just shock).
   d. What are thought-provoking poems? How do ideas in poems affect us? Are they just thoughts or can they make us feel? If so, how?

   e. What causes humor? What makes a poem amusing? Subject, words, images, etc.?
2. Discuss how the poems make you feel. What emotions are evoked?
3. Discuss what the poems mean. What primary or literal meanings do you see? What other meanings do you see (figurative, metaphoric, symbolic)? Consider as many interpretations as meaningfully possible.
4. Try to reach consensus. After discussion, select the poem most exemplary in your given category. Consider: Why is this poem the best choice?

I circulate around the room as an advisor. What a joy to sit with five students discussing reactions to poems! Students often ask my opinion—"Is this poem shocking?"—or hope that I will be an arbiter—"We can't choose between these two; what do you think?" I actively listen, but refrain from the posture of authority. I want the students to gain confidence in their own judgments. At times, I ask provocative questions to help them explicate, interpret, or express an opinion. I ask them to point to particular images, words, or phrases to support their point of view. I might suggest another pertinent poem to consider. And in the end, I reserve final approval of all choices, ensuring that no two groups select the same poem and that the poems selected are appropriate. At the conclusion of the first class, I collect their papers and tally the independent selections for future consideration.

On the second day of the small-group discussions, I distribute guidelines for oral presentations. I tell the students to consider the following instructions after they have selected the poem they will present to the group as a whole.

Oral Presentation Guide Sheet

Directions: Each member of the group must have an oral role. Divide the following tasks among your group members. Everyone in the group is responsible for the entire report. Know what others are going to do and say in case of absenteeism.

1. Read your poem aloud to the class. Read it to make sense; read it to make a dramatic or powerful presentation. Practice several readings before your presentation.
2. Define the nature of your category. Explain to the class the criteria you used to select your poem.
3. Explain the meaning of the poem. You may consider a primary and then a greater meaning if you want. Offer several interpretations when appropriate. Do you see any figurative or symbolic meanings?
4. Point to any particular poetic devices that may explain the meaning of your poem or its emotional effect. Identify relevant images, sound devices, lines, figures of speech, etc.

5. Explain why the poem was selected and what other poems were considered and rejected.

Lesson Four: Panel Presentations and Large-Group Discussions (3–4) Days

In the large-group presentations, we share as a class our understanding, interpretation, and appreciation of poetry. To ensure active listening and audience participation, after each poetic presentation I call for "poem challenges." Anyone in the audience may challenge the presenters with a poem they feel equal or more exemplary than the one offered. In this way, we expand the number of poems under consideration. There is a high level of excitement as the groups report, for all students are curious to hear the selections and to see how the selections compare with their own choices. I am pleased that students have chosen poems I would have selected as ideal for study.

The shocking group, for example, presents two choices of equal value and interest: "Richard Cory" by Edwin Arlington Robinson and "Death of the Ball Turret Gunner" by Randall Jarrell. The students suggest that the shocking effect of "Richard Cory" lies in its surprising and ironic ending—despite his riches, he kills himself; thus the shock of the unexpected. They further explain the shock they feel from the surprising and repellent final image of the dead soldier in "Death of the Ball Turret Gunner." They conclude both poems are shocking, but in different ways. There is an air of great respect and appreciation as the class as a whole agrees with the value and meaning of these selections. Then a poem challenge is offered by a member of the audience: Robert Frost's "Out, Out—." I ask the challenger to read the poem aloud for consideration, then explain its meaning and shock value. The challenger contends that "Out, Out—" is surprising, ironic in its ending, and repellent in the image of the boy's mutilated hand. The point of such debate is not, of course, to promote competition or the attitude that one poem is "better" than another. The challenges simply provide an enjoyable way of discussing and sharing more poems of comparable value. Students find the challenges stimulating and in the spirit of good fun. I allow the challenges to continue as interest prevails.

The following poems are frequently selected and presented by students for each of the other categories:

> Beautiful Poems: "Stars" by Sara Teasdale; "Lilacs" by Amy Lowell; "Stopping by Woods on a Snowy Evening" by Robert Frost; "The Blindman" by May Swenson

Emotive Poems: "Too Blue" by Langston Hughes; "Lament" by Edna St. Vincent Millay; "Patterns" by Amy Lowell; "Auto Wreck" by Karl Shapiro; "Go Down Death" by James Weldon Johnson

Thought-Provoking Poems: "The Red Wheelbarrow" by William Carlos Williams; "The Skater of Ghost Lake" by William Benet; "Mirror" by Sylvia Plath; "Beware: Do Not Read This Poem" by Ishmael Reed

Humorous Poems: "Dick Szymanski" by Ogden Nash; "Fish Story" by Richard Armour

After several days of presentation, our class has discussed, interpreted, and appreciated in-depth at least ten poems. We have developed a sense of shared values and expectations, as well as an emerging aesthetic sensibility. The final lesson in this unit attempts to extend and develop this poetic appreciation.

Lesson Five: Writing a Poetry Paper/Writing Original Poetry

At the conclusion of all the presentations, I point out that our study of twentieth-century American poetry has been limited so far to the available textbooks. Now I ask the students to further extend and develop their appreciation by searching for their "favorite" poet or type of poetry. I suggest they browse through local libraries and bookstores for individual collections and anthologies of contemporary poets. I distribute the following assignment.

Writing a Poetry Paper

Directions: Search through anthologies and individual collections of twentieth-century American poetry for your favorite poet or type of poetry. Select three poems by one poet or three poems by several poets on a similar topic to compare and contrast. Choose poems that affect you strongly, poems you understand and have something to say about. These poems should inspire you and provoke thinking. In this sense, they might be called your "favorite" poems. When you have selected your favorite poet or poems, develop a thesis by considering one of the following approaches:

1. Read the poetry of a particular type of poet or class of poetry you might prefer: women poets, anti-war poets, veterans; ethnic poetry (Black, Jewish, Chinese, American Indian, etc.), prison poetry, religious poetry, etc.
2. Read poetry involving a subject you might prefer: nature, animals, flying, sports, friendship, separation, love, death, suicide, childhood, etc.

3. Continue to search for the most shocking, beautiful, thought-provoking, or emotive poems.

   Write a three-page paper explaining what the poems mean to you and why they are your favorites. When you are finished, write three or more of your own original poems inspired from your favorite poems or poet. You might be inspired by the language, the subject, or style of the poems. Let this be reflected in your own poetry. Bring to class your favorite poems and your original poetry. Be prepared to share these with the class.

Our final class session reflects the success of our many weeks of aesthetic study. We sit seminar style as each student reads a favorite poem to the class and then explains the reasons for selection. Students are attentive, highly focused, and respectful of their fellow poets. After weeks of exploring our aesthetic sensibilities, students amaze each other with powerful, inspired, original poetry. My students have certainly learned to appreciate poetry, and I, in many ways, have begun to realize my fantasy.

In conclusion, the strategy presented in this chapter enables students to respond in ways that:

1. Engage them emotionally (sensually/imaginatively)—*what* is the dominant emotional effect of the text on you?
2. Create personal awareness and insight—*why* does the text have that effect?
3. Illuminate the text—*how* does the text cause the effect?
4. Foster participation in the art form.

I believe this approach balances the need to understand and make sense of the text—the basic goal of any literature course—with the need to engage the student/reader in personal, pleasurable appreciation.

Note

1. I am indebted to David Swanger, *The Poem as Process* (1974) for this aesthetic view of poetry. Swanger places himself in the tradition of Coleridge, Beardsley, Ogden and Richards, and Susanne Langer. He develops a poetic that views poetry as evocative, empathetic, and experiential. He contends that poetry suggests, evokes, and inspires the interplay of attitudes and emotions; from this interplay comes the reader's meaning as well as the poet's. Thus, the reader becomes in a sense a "co-poet," creating the poem anew in the process of

perception and response. This approach, coupled with the reader-response theory of Louise Rosenblatt, provides the foundation for the teaching strategy offered here.

References

Levy, Wilbert, editor. 1979. *Poems: American Themes.* New York: AMSCO Publications.

Swanger, David. 1974. *The Poem as Process.* New York: Harcourt Brace Jovanovich Inc.

Weimer, David, editor. 1973. *20th Century American Poetry: Landscapes of the Mind* ("America" series). Evanston, Ill.: McDougal, Littell, Inc.

6 "Stopping by Woods on a Snowy Evening": A Classroom Experiment in Literary Response

Mary Alice Delia
Seneca Valley High School
Germantown, Maryland

> "A good man's son, obeying wisdom's words,
> You'd scarcely find grown bad. But yet you would
> Never by *teaching* make the bad man good."
>
> —Theognis of Megara, 6th century, B.C.

When high school students tell us they don't like to read and that poetry is "boring," perhaps—instead of gnashing our teeth—we should listen to them! Clearly, if students find "dull and boring" the very poems we most admire, something is dreadfully wrong—if not with the poems, then with the way we are presenting them. In presenting poetry to a class of average-level seniors, I decided to focus on the student as the source of "meaning" instead of myself as an "authority." I wanted students to experience reading literature from opposing and equally valid points of view. Before I could do any of this, however, I had to change the "rules" of the classroom. I had to convince students that although I described myself as a teacher, I did not believe that literature could be taught; that literature—in my opinion—contained no "deep, eternal meaning," that its "truth" must be created each day, anew. For students long-accustomed to thinking of poems as problems or puzzles to be solved, however, this message—as I soon discovered—proved terrifyingly new!

"No Such Thing as Teaching"

As Shoshana Felman (1982) observes, Socrates, the first pedagogue, begins his teaching by "asserting not just his own ignorance, but the radical impossibility of teaching" itself. Asked by the wealthy nobleman Menon to teach him how to acquire virtue, Socrates reprimands his would-be pupil: "You are a young rogue," Socrates scolds, for "now you ask me if I can teach you, when I tell you there is no such thing as teaching, only remembering" (Rouse 1956, 42).

Since I, too, wanted to inaugurate my course by throwing the "scene" of teaching into radical doubt, we began by reading aloud this dialogue between Socrates and Menon, stopping frequently to interrogate its propositions.

"Is Socrates right?" I asked, "'If there are neither teachers nor learners of any given thing,' then it 'cannot be taught'?"

"Yes," the students immediately agreed. "Socrates is right."

"Then poetry is a subject that can be taught simply because I am here as a teacher of poetry, and because you are here as students? It has no greater 'truth'?"

Twenty-eight pairs of eyes squinted suspiciously. What sort of subversive proposition was *this*?

"Or is it the other way around? That if neither you nor I were here, the 'truth' of Shakespeare's great poems would still exist somewhere—*out there!*"

Yes and *no* answers mingled. "What does she mean, 'Out there'?" The students could not decide.

"Well, make up your minds!" I commanded. "You can't have it both ways. Do we teach things because they are 'true'? Or do we *make* things 'true' by teaching them?"

A few moments of stunned silence—then order quickly broke down as the students vied for attention. "What about math? Aren't numbers 'true'? Why did *you* go to college? What about history? Why are you *doing* this to us? How should *we* know?" And finally, the inevitable, "What do *you* think?"

As an answer to all these questions, I slipped a Greek tunic over my head and hung around my neck a sign that said "Socrates." "What in the world is wrong with *you?*" I scolded, recalling Socrates' admonition to Menon, "that you come here today asking me to 'teach'?"

Needless to say, the students loved the performance and thereafter displayed at least a healthy skepticism toward poetry as a subject to be studied for its "eternal truth." This budding new doubt of knowledge as something "fixed in the stars," however, did not extend to the pedagogue as site of authority. No matter how vigorously I tried to decenter myself, the students still depended on me to resolve, explicate, and explain. Breaking them of this long-standing habit was indeed difficult. Emphatically I did *not* want to make poetry "true" by teaching it, nor did I intend to teach poetry as though it were "true"! What I wanted was something entirely different—not the truth of the poem (for to whom is it given?), but the truth of the poem to my teenage students. I wanted these seventeen-year-olds to respond to poetry just as naturally as they responded to other events in their lives, to read poetry with the same eyes as they read all other writing, not as something specialized, formal, and discrete! Too many years of analyzing, however, had convinced them otherwise: the language of poetry, in their long-suffering view, like the language of computers, was something that had to be studied, worried over, dissected, and learned.

Poetry as Discourse

Finally, I decided to focus my efforts on the reading of a single poem, Frost's "Stopping by Woods on a Snowy Evening"—probably the most anthologized lyric in American literature, and unfortunately, one of the most widely "taught." The meaning of Frost's poem, like the meaning of all literature, depends entirely on one's ideological point of view. And rather than impose someone else's interpretation on the students, I wanted to help them discover their own ideological convictions, to find issues in the poem that concerned them, to read the poem from the standpoint of their own problems, values, and beliefs! All this would be possible, I reasoned, if they could stop looking at the poem as literature and begin responding to it as discourse, as language open to "feedback" within the context of their lives.

Poetry when read aloud, however, tends to sound like "poetry." Following the first reading of Frost's poem, the students maintained a studied silence.

"Well," I asked encouragingly, "who wants to comment?"

"It's a nice poem," a student finally volunteered. "I like it. But I'm not sure exactly what it means."

"It doesn't mean anything!" I exploded. "The source of its meaning lies entirely within *you!* Think of yourself as a *person,* not as a student. How do certain lines or phrases make you *feel?* To what would you like to respond?"

"Well," the student continued, ignoring my outburst altogether, "what *I* get from it is that we never take time out to enjoy nature, like to 'watch the woods fill up with snow.' We're always too busy . . ."

Heads bobbed up and down, guiltily. Here was a message from literature the students had heard before!

"But what's so great about watching the woods fill up with snow?" I challenged. "Be honest! Wouldn't most of you rather be with your friends talking or listening to music?"

Quick, surprised flashes of assent. I had scored a bull's-eye!

"Good!" I congratulated them. "I wouldn't believe you if you said otherwise! Now, stop trying to get something *from* the poem! Believe me, there is nothing *in* the poem to get, nothing you can scratch like an instant lottery ticket and find, nothing you can make fall out if you shake it hard! Instead, try to open the poem up and insert something of yourselves *into* it! Are there no words or lines in the poem that you can relate to honestly, without trying to sound like English students?"

The students considered. Finally, someone broke the ice. "To me, the poem is mainly about promises. I like the way the guy says he's going to keep his promises. I can relate to that. I hate people who make promises and don't keep them."

Enthusiastically, another student broke in: "Yeah, my dad's a prime example. He promised a long time ago he would get me a car for graduation, and now he's trying to back out of the deal. And it's not money, either. He's got the money. But all of a sudden, he's giving me all this crap about working for it myself."

From around the room, I heard appreciative murmurs of recognition. "That's what I hate about people, too," a student quickly empathized. "For instance, my mom told me that if I got straight Bs last semester, I could go to school out of state. Well, I worked my *butt* off. I mean, I gave up *everything*, including my part-time job, and I did it! I got four *B*s and one *A*, but now she's backing down. She says it's too far to go, that she'll miss me too much. What I want to know is—why did she promise me in the first place? Don't you think that's a bit unfair?"

Without comment, I turned the student's question back to the class. "How do some of the rest of you feel?" I asked, noting at least fifteen hands waving in the air.

For the next half hour, the students shared stories, clarified problems, sought advice, and generally opened up. They spoke of promises made and broken by parents, siblings, friends, employers, even teachers. Some of the stories were light-hearted and funny; others, downright sad, even tragic. One boy, for instance, told of getting his father's promise to stop smoking, but not in time to save him from dying of lung cancer. Another student spoke of the anger she had felt when a teacher betrayed her promise to give her some extra help. Clearly, this was a topic the entire class could respond to and discuss honestly—not as an idea *in* the poem, but as an idea taken *from* the poem and contextualized within the experience of real life!

Responses to literature need not be based on the reading of a poem as a unified whole. What is important, if we want students to connect with literature, is that they find in it something to pull out and *talk* about, something of genuine interest to them as teenagers. Through sharing their feelings, they do forge strong and lasting bonds, not only with the poems and stories we'd like them to read, but also with each other—through the texts they inscribe as they speak.

All this I pointed out to the students. "Do you understand now," I asked, "that to take control of your own reading experience, you have only to open and read the poem from your personal point of view?"

"But what if we miss something important?"

"What you don't 'see'," I assured them, "you can't possibly 'miss.' Poems, after all, yield many 'talking points.' Some simply may not be available to you until later, when you've gathered more life experience."

"But suppose there's absolutely nothing in the poem to talk about?" they worried.

"Then rewrite it," I suggested. "Read it from right to left, bottom to top. Substitute words. Add to it. Invent your own connections. Do whatever it takes to make the poem come to you!"

Gradually, the students came to believe and trust me, and throughout our study of poetry, I held to my word. I never insisted that they memorize and feed back the English major's "received" version of any poem, but only that each student engage it meaningfully in terms of his or her lived experience. When students feel free to interpret literature in the same way as they are certainly free to interpret and comment on other events in their lives, they approach it quite positively, as a way of talking about each other and themselves. Which is another way of saying, of course, that one good use of literature is to affirm and validate life.

Reading Poetry from Another's Viewpoint

By the end of the first three weeks, the students had almost completely taken over the class, articulating for each new poem their own topics and discussing them with growing enthusiasm and confidence. It is not enough, however, that students learn to read literature from the viewpoint of their own social and cultural background, although that is where interpretation must always begin. They must also learn to read as the "other," as persons whose social, economic, and cultural backgrounds differ most radically from their own. To read literature against the background of one's own experience is the first goal; to deny other readings, however, is not only socially and ethically irresponsible, it is privileging one's own point of view above all others. In reading as "other," we not only extend literature as discourse, we acknowledge that each of us reads differently, depending on our psychological makeup, sex, race, age, economic class, social position, and even our spiritual or philosophical point of view.

To learn to read as the "other," we turned again to Frost's poem, this time to view it through different eyes. I wanted each student to read the poem imaginatively from the perspective of at least one of the following groups: the homeless, blacks, and gays. Dividing the class into three groups, I asked each group to respond orally to the following questions:

1. How well do you know the man in the village who owns the woods?
2. Why are you traveling on the darkest evening of the year?
3. What are the promises you have to keep?
4. How would you re-title this poem?

While the students' responses contained many stereotypes and generalizations, they nonetheless demonstrated how differently each of us reads literature, depending on our background, and how wrong (in my opinion) we are to force a single, transcendent truth upon any text, no matter how classic or venerable its status. The homeless, for example, were traveling on the "darkest evening of the year" because they had no place to call their own, no place to sleep; they also, sadly, had no "promises to keep." They knew the owner of the woods by name only; presumably, he had no knowledge of them. This group titled the poem "Invisibility."

The blacks, on the other hand, were traveling to escape oppression. They knew the man who owned the woods, but they expected no help from him because he was white. They were tired of fighting for equal rights and wanted to stop and enjoy the beauty of the snow-filled woods, but they had promised to keep going until their struggle against racism and discrimination was won. As a title, they suggested "Our Day Will Come."

Like the blacks, the gays had been discriminated against; they had also been ridiculed and victimized by the straight people in the village, especially by the man who owned the woods. Tired and discouraged, they wanted to give up, to enter the woods, lie down, and die, but they had promised to help each other survive. They titled the poem, "Someday, You'll Understand."

What I found fascinating about these responses was that in each, the script reflected understanding of hardship and deprivation. The blacks had been oppressed; the gays humiliated and ridiculed; the homeless cast out. Clearly the students had confronted the "other"; as predominantly white, mainstream, middle-class adolescents, they had located their own differences from the marginalized and had described how these differences might result in new readings of the poem. And interestingly, the only subgroup to see a death wish in the poem was the group of gays. This group's ability to construct a death wish, it seems to me, reveals not so much literary skill as empathy with the plight of other human beings. To John Ciardi's question, "How does the poem mean," the students might well respond: "By putting oneself in another's shoes."

Near the end of the course, we returned once again to Frost's poem; this time, I asked each student to reread it, individually, and then to write an essay in response. Nearly all the essays described vivid, personal responses to the poem—and not necessarily those the students had explored earlier. The students were now preparing to graduate; some were filled with trepidation and anxiety, others seemed to drift away on pink clouds of speculation. Now, however, they wrote of their own "promises to keep," their own desires to fulfill not only the expectations of their parents, but obligations to themselves as well. And then, a heartstopper. Over half the students included in their promises lifelong commitments to helping "others." These students, it seems to me, are not only out of the woods, they are traveling on the road we all want them to go. They are reading the poem alone now, and they are reading it well.

For high school students, the value of literature lies precisely in its ability to inspire strong *new* readings based on multiple, even opposing, points of view. Literature, after all, is not something we want students simply to appreciate; it is something we want them to enter as discourse, as language through which they can build powerful connections—not only to their own everyday lives, but to the lives of "others."

References

Felman, Shoshana. 1982. Psychoanalysis and Education: Teaching Terminable and Interminable. *Yale French Studies* 63: 21–44.

Rouse, W. H. D., editor. 1956. *Great Dialogues of Plato.* New York: New American Library.

7 Making Sense of Poetry through Constructing, Collaborating, and Imitating

Jeff Golub
Shorecrest High School
Seattle, Washington

An important goal when discussing and analyzing poetry in class is to make students responsible for their own meanings. Students should be able to create and explain their own meaning for a poem, support their interpretation with references from the text, and respond intelligently to their classmates' perceptions and interpretations. Such competence, however, does not develop when the students are forced to discover a predetermined meaning imposed on the poem by the teacher. Students find their own meanings by constructing questions, collaborating on answers, and imitating the poet's style.

Too often teachers play the game of "guess-what's-in-my-mind," asking questions for which they already have "correct" answers in mind. Asking questions about poetry is important, but it is *students* who should be asking the questions as they seek to construct meanings. They should then collaborate with classmates to articulate their responses to those questions. The following activity provides a structure for this process:

1. Introduce a poem to the class by first reading it aloud. Poems are meant to be heard as well as seen.
2. Immediately ask students to write down three questions they have about the poem. These can be questions about a certain word ("What does this word mean?" "Why does the poet use this word here?"), a phrase, or a whole section.
3. After the questions have been written, direct the students to form themselves into small groups, four or five people in each group. Then instruct the students to work within their groups to generate answers to their questions.

This procedure has several advantages over a more traditional, teacher-led discussion: students are encouraged to ask their own questions of the poem instead of simply responding to the teacher's questions; this process uses students' talk as a vehicle for learning, allowing students to try out emerging ideas on each other; and a collaborative approach is used to generate individual meanings and insights.

At the end of the small-group discussions, a recorder appointed for each group should summarize for the whole class what questions were brought up and what responses were generated. The entire class might then work together to provide additional responses and interpretations for those questions that a particular group found difficult to handle. You should find that, at the end of this process, the students will have covered—or more important, *un*covered—most of the points and parts of the poem that you, the teacher, would have discussed anyway. And they will have done it in a way that makes sense to them and allows them to make sense of the poem.

Sometimes students can respond to a poem not by analyzing it, but by imitating its structure and content. One poem that invites this kind of response is William Stafford's "Fifteen."

Fifteen

South of the bridge on Seventeenth
I found back of the willows one summer
day a motorcycle with engine running
as it lay on its side, ticking over
slowly in the high grass. I was fifteen.

I admired all that pulsing gleam, the
shiny flanks, the demure headlights
fringed where it lay; I led it gently
to the road and stood with that
companion, ready and friendly. I was fifteen.

We could find the end of a road, meet
the sky on out Seventeenth. I thought about
hills, and patting the handle got back a
confident opinion. On the bridge we indulged
a forward feeling, a tremble. I was fifteen.

Thinking, back farther in the grass I found
the owner, just coming to, where he had flipped
over the rail. He had blood on his hand, was pale—
I helped him walk to his machine. He ran his hand
over it, called me good man, roared away.

I stood there, fifteen.

After reading the poem aloud, discuss the structure and content. Notice that in the first stanza, the speaker in the poem simply reports an incident: he finds an overturned motorcycle by the side of the road. In the second stanza, he responds to the look and feel of the machine, and in the third stanza he begins to imagine and fantasize about what it might be like to own and ride it. The events in the last stanza, however, bring him back sharply to reality.

Invite students to write a poem that imitates this structure, but have them change the age of the character. For instance:

Ninety

> In the nursing-home cafeteria during lunch-time, I gazed out the window at a group of school-children running and playing "Follow-the-Leader" in the distant meadow. I was ninety.
>
> I loved their laughter and the way they ran in circles and jumped and fell down and then got up again to run some more. They were having a *lot* of fun. I was ninety.
>
> I could lead those children on a merry chase and play "Hide-'n'-Go-Seek" and tell stories just like I did so many years ago. I want to do that again. I was ninety.
>
> Turning away from the window at last, I found that my mashed potatoes were cold and hard and the gravy was lumpy. But it was OK. I couldn't finish them anyway because the nurse came up to me and said that lunch-time was over and it was time for me to be wheeled back to my room.
>
> I sat there, ninety.

Notice how the imitation follows the same structure as the original, mimicking the progression of the character's thoughts and contrasting those feelings and fantasies with the reality of the situation in the last stanza. Another imitation has an interesting twist at the end:

Five

> I was playing in the yard. It was sunny and I built a neet-o sandcastle in my sandbox. I could see the older kids waiting for the school bus for kindergarten. I was five.
>
> I wanted to play with them. They were so lucky because they were six and they got to go to school with all of their friends. The bus came, so I stood and ran to the fence. "Hey! What about me?" I was five.
>
> If I could go, I'd show them. I'd play with all the toys and meet new friends. I could be just like all the other kids. Still, I was five.

The bus left without me. The bus-driver didn't even wave. Then I could hear my mom calling me. She told me to stay away from the fence. So I turned back to my sandbox.

I kicked my stupid old sandcastle. I hate being five.

Another poem that lends itself to imitation is "April" by Marcia Lee Masters, a celebration of that month that is filled with vivid, characteristic images.

April

It's lemonade, it's lemonade, it's daisy.
It's a roller-skating, scissor-grinding day;
It's gingham-waisted, chocolate flavored, lazy,
With the children flower-scattered at their play.

It's the sun like watermelon,
And the sidewalks overlaid
With a glaze of yellow yellow
Like a jar of marmalade.

It's the mower gently mowing,
And the stars like startled glass,
While the mower keeps on going
Through a waterfall of grass.

Then the rich magenta evening
Like a sauce upon the walk,
And the porches softly swinging
With a hammockful of talk.

It's the hobo at the corner
With his lilac-sniffing gait,
And the shy departing thunder
Of the fast departing skate.

It's lemonade, it's lemonade, it's April!
A water sprinkler, puddle winking time,
When a boy who peddles slowly, with a smile remote and holy,
Sells you April chocolate flavored for a dime.

Invite students to imitate the first stanza but have them change the month. A student who writes about December, then, would not use the image, "It's lemonade, it's lemonade," but might change it to something more appropriate: "It's Santa Claus, it's Santa Claus, it's holly." By substituting images appropriate for the month they have selected, students come to see both the structure and craft involved in the original. Here is a more complete sample imitation:

October

It's pumpkins, it's pumpkins, it's leaves.
It's a costume-wearing, monster-making fright.
It's rainy-weathered, cloudy-covered, freezing,
With the homes candy-gathered through the night.

Finally, students can write their own apology, imitating William Carlos Williams's poem, "This Is Just to Say." First, the original:

This Is Just to Say

I have eaten
the plums
that were in
the icebox

and which
you were probably
saving
for breakfast

Forgive me
they were delicious
so sweet
and so cold

And now a sample imitation:

This Is Just to Say

I have looked at
the math problems
that were in
your notebook

and which
you had certainly
worked hard on
to arrive at the answers.

Forgive me
they were needed
so easy to get to
and so correct

Making sense of poetry is a meaning-making process, and these activities can help in this effort. They involve students in asking questions of poems, constructing appropriate and insightful responses in collaboration with classmates, and imitating the structure and content of poems. Through these activities, students make sense of poems in ways that make sense to them.

---

8 Literature on the Screen: Film Adaptations in the Classroom

Peter S. Gardner
Berklee College of Music

In a recent evaluation of my freshman introduction to literature class, a student commented on the three film adaptations of short stories we had seen during the semester: "The films were definitely one of the best parts of the course. They made me go back and reread the short stories in a totally new light. The discussions were some of the most interesting we had all semester." Films often draw students into lively debate about artistic intent and elicit response from even the most reticent students. Some teachers may regard the viewing of screen adaptations as a threat to engaged critical readings of texts. This has not been my experience. I have found screen adaptations not a substitute for academic rigor, but a powerful tool in helping students to interact with literature, discuss literary concepts, and develop logical and critical thinking skills.

Rather than diverting attention from literary works, films can serve as a springboard for discussion, focusing fresh attention on the works themselves. They often send students back to the original text excited about new and closer analysis; they encourage such active, and interactive, reading skills as asking questions, making and confirming predictions, formulating hypotheses, and revising interpretations. Films can also help students develop logical and critical thinking skills, such as comparing and contrasting, making inferences, evaluating intentions, and forming critical judgments that go beyond initial response. Equally important, discussing film adaptations encourages students to think creatively by assuming the role of film director and imagining what they would have done differently.

Many of my students tend to view literature "horizontally," focusing primarily on plot movement and isolating general themes. They are not used to considering the relationship between content and form or regarding theme as being integrally connected to, and developed through, the setting, imagery, point of view, tone, and other literary devices. Concentrating on similarities and differences between screen adaptations and their original texts can draw students into the "vertical" or polyphonic texture of much literature and help them discover connections between theme, structure, and style.

I have often heard teachers say that they would like to use film adaptations of literary works, but that these simply take too much time. I would point out, however, that alternatives exist to watching feature-length films; for example, there are many thirty- to sixty-minute adaptations of short stories and short novels that can be shown in one class and discussed in the next.[1] I have also found it effective to show only part of a feature-length film, such as the first or second half.

The way I usually approach film adaptations is to have students read the literary work first, view the film, and then explore similarities and differences in theme, structure, and style. We discuss what has been kept the same (plot elements, characters, setting, and so on), and what has been changed (added, deleted, expanded, and deemphasized). Our attention continually turns back to the original as we discuss the effects of such changes. Why, for example, does the director make these changes? What is the relationship between the author's original intent and the director's artistic license? As author or director, what would you do differently?

Comparing the Short Story to the Screen Adaptation

In order to show more specifically how a film adaptation can be used in a literature class, I would like to turn to a version of William Faulkner's frequently anthologized short story, "A Rose for Emily."† By focusing on the relationship between the story and the film, especially on a number of significant differences, and describing the types of issues we typically explore in class, I hope to illustrate how a screen adaptation can engage students in the fabric of an original text and encourage the intellectual skills I mentioned earlier.

We usually start by discussing similarities between the short story and screen adaptation. Unlike most screen adaptations which diminish the role of the literary narrator and incorporate that person's observations into the action or dialogue of the film, this one retains a

† The film adaptation I am discussing, *A Rose for Emily*, was directed in 1983 by Lyndon Chubbuck, runs twenty-seven minutes, stars Anjelica Huston, and is narrated by John Houseman. The distributor is Pyramid Film and Video, Santa Monica, California.

narrator throughout, who functions similarly to the one in the story. As in the story, characters speak very little in the film, and the narrator selects statements from the text—occasionally reordering them, placing ones early in the story later in the film and ones later in the story early in the film—to describe the characters as they progress through the plot.

In both media a nonparticipatory omniscient narrator speaks for the entire town, using *we* in a detached yet occasionally gossipy manner. The narrator in both formats expresses an ambivalent attitude towards Emily, at times genuinely sympathizing with her and feeling proud to have her as a "monument" to a rapidly fading genteel past, and at times feeling superior to her and viewing her as an anachronism so as to vindicate an increasingly "modern" lifestyle. We discuss where this ambivalent stance of the narrator—regarding Emily as both idol and scapegoat—is revealed in the story and in the film.

We then go on to briefly consider several other similarities. These include the geographic and temporal settings, which are the same; Emily's and Homer Barron's appearance, which is usually as students had imagined; and a general atmosphere of mystery, foreboding, and decay. Both the story and the film incorporate the usual Gothic trappings: dusty hallways, shadowy landscapes, a mysterious silent servant, a madwoman, a hideous secret, a murder, a corpse. The film, however, replaces the typical crumbling mansion with an immaculately well-kept Georgian house. We speculate about why the director retained the stylish and highly ornamented house of Emily's youth throughout the film, rather than showing the change to a dilapidated structure as in the story.

After touching on the basic similarities between the story and the film, we spend most of our time focusing on the significant differences between the two. I start by asking students what they consider effective changes in the film. One of the issues that usually comes up first, on which students are inevitably divided, is the development of Emily's father and of Homer Barron in the film. Both characters are shown in scenes not appearing in the story that emphasize their coarse, egotistical natures. Near the beginning of the film, for example, we see the father roaring drunk, brandishing a sword, and bellowing Civil War stories, and later at dinner castigating Emily for apparently asking him about a wedding dress. Homer Barron similarly appears in several scenes that highlight his insensitivity and hedonist disregard for Emily. We see him, for instance, responding to Emily's remark that her father had just died: "Let's go. It's nice out." And later we watch him seducing Emily, guzzling a drink with one hand while removing her clothes with the other.

Many students feel that the scenes in the film between Emily and her father provide us with a more vivid picture of her "vanquished" youth than in the story, and thus a clearer motivation for her subsequent vanquishing of all visitors to the house, and ultimately of Homer Barron. Other students find the scenes unnecessary and even detractive, maintaining that Faulkner's brief portrayal of Emily and her father in the imagined "tableau" of the townspeople gives the reader a powerful sense of their relationship, and at the same time leaves something to the imagination: "We had long thought of them as a tableau, Miss Emily a slender figure in white in the background, her father a spraddled silhouette in the foreground, his back to her and clutching a horsewhip, the two of them framed by the back-flung door." Many students find the striking contrast between the "slender figure in white" and the "spraddled silhouette" more potent than all of the father's ranting in the film, and the connotations of the onomatopoeic "spraddled" equally, if not more, evocative.

Perhaps the greatest difference between the story and the film involves the antitheses that run through the story on a number of different levels. We see these, for example, in Faulkner's ambivalence towards the South, which is downplayed in the film, and in much of the imagery, such as the vivid contrast between Emily the "monument" and the "slender figure in white" and the polarities at the end in the "huge meadow" versus the "narrow bottleneck," and the "grimace of love." The film deemphasizes many of the central conflicts of the story: North versus South, past versus present, and tradition versus change. The story traces these conflicts in Emily's own life and in the society around her; one parallels and enhances the other. By exploring interconnections between levels of antithesis in the story as reflected in the theme, character description, tone, and imagery, and having the film as a sharp contrast where most of these antitheses are deemphasized, students are drawn into the multilayered texture of the original.

The story also employs considerably more understatement than the film, especially regarding Emily's motivation for killing Homer Barron. We see the film's preference for explicit statement in the narrator, who usually uses Faulkner's exact words, but at times substitutes his own more direct ones. I ask students to try to notice when this occurs and to speculate about the director's intention. Many students, for example, comment on the different descriptions of Homer Barron's desertion of Emily. The film narrator remarks, "Miss Emily had become a tragic focal point, now hopelessly and disastrously compromised." The narrator seems to feel a need to supply a probable motivation for Emily's killing Homer Barron by underlining the humiliation she must have experienced after Homer jilted her. Faulkner, on the other hand, merely writes, "So we were not surprised when Homer Barron—the streets had been finished some time since—was gone." Emily's compromised position remains unstated yet implied. By considering the definitiveness of many of the film narrator's remarks, and his tendency to comment on events rather than simply describe them and let viewers draw their own conclusions, students gain an appreciation of Faulkner's subtlety and art of indirection.

The film's frequent commenting on events reflects a tendency to make explicit several possible explanations for Emily's monstrous behavior, which are left nebulous in the story. Students usually notice right away, for example, the different emphasis placed on Emily's crazy great-aunt, "old lady Wyatt." Faulkner makes only two brief references to this woman who "had gone completely crazy at last," and there is only the slightest hint that Emily might have inherited her insanity. The film, on the other hand, heightens this possibility. Near the beginning, for instance, we see Emily's Aunt Wyatt (no longer a great-aunt but now a closer relation, her father's sister) come running down the stairs in her bathrobe, yelling, "Emily, hide the silver! The Yankees. They're here. They're coming!" Although the townspeople in both the story and the film are reluctant to attribute Emily's behavior to insanity, in the film they seem more willing to entertain the possibility.

The film also adds a scene highlighting Emily's apparent suicidal inclinations. Shortly after her father's death, we see Emily standing in front of a mirror, looking extremely distraught and holding a straight-edge razor. Just as she makes the slightest movement of the razor towards herself, a tremendous explosion shakes the whole house, and she rushes downstairs to find Homer Barron repaving the sidewalks. The added scenes, one suggesting insanity and this one severe emotional instability, usually lead to a lively discussion of Emily's motivation for committing acts of murder and necrophilia.

A final instance of the film's preference for explicit reference, which students almost always comment on, is the symbolism of the rose. Faulkner consciously avoids references to actual flowers and provides only the slightest hint of them at the end with Emily's "curtains of faded rose color" and "rose-shaded lights." The film, on the other hand, brings the image of the rose to the foreground. We see Emily several times with a rose in her hair and pinned to her dress, the outline of a large rose stenciled onto the upper glass of her front door, and a Confederate soldier placing a long-stemmed red rose on her corpse during the funeral near the end. We discuss the difference between the literal presentation of the rose in the film and the metaphorical one in the story.

Our focus on particular points of similarity and difference between the story and the film culminates in students' overall impressions of the two. Many feel that the film is a successful Gothic horror tale that gives us a graphic picture of the isolated life of a Southern belle, her dominating father, and a fun-loving but insensitive Northerner who jilts her. We explore, however, the argument that despite these effective portrayals, the film ultimately remains an old-fashioned thriller without the historical perspective or emotional depth of the original. We consider whether the film prepares us adequately for the ending; that is, whether the horror and madness revealed in the final scene are sufficiently motivated so that the film does not remain a clinical case study of a psychotic woman, but rather a rich social and psychological commentary surrounding an irrevocable tragedy, as in the story.

We examine the contention that Emily's hideous deeds in the story, as opposed to the film, are motivated by her character—by a series of consistent reactions to people and events. Her blurred distinction between illusion and reality (an obsession with an irretrievable past and a denial of time and death), and adamant resistance to change of all kinds and to ordinary standards of behavior, lead inexorably to her monstrous acts. It is precisely the lack of these consistent character traits in the film that makes the final revelation ultimately gratuitous. Focusing on such issues as consistency of character reaction, the extent to which the author and the director comply with Gothic convention and go beyond it, and their intent in both media helps students develop an ability to form critical judgments based on supportable criteria.

Finally, we discuss whether the film adaptation incorporates the tragic and heroic framework of the original. Most students come to the conclusion that the film deals successfully with the sterile relationship between Emily and the male world surrounding her, but does not explore the elements of tragedy that raise the story above one of personal woe: Emily's excessive pride, her fierce independence and indomitable will, and her heroic attempt to transcend ordinary values, time, and death. The film sends students back to the story, searching for clues to Emily's universal downfall.

A film adaptation can draw students into the texture of a literary work and help them focus on, and discover relationships between, its elements. I am always searching for ways to engage students in lively discussions of literature and literary concepts that help them appreciate what at times seems esoteric. Film adaptations can assist in this pursuit. They provide a forum for students to share responses to works of art and enhance students' ability to think creatively, logically, and critically.

Note

1. For the most comprehensive listing of programs currently available on video (including film adaptations of short stories, novels, and plays), see *The Video Source Book,* 10th edition, edited by David J. Weiner (1988, Detroit: Gale Research). This publication lists films alphabetically with producer, distributor, release date, running time, brief description of plot, and intended audience. It can be found in the reference section of most libraries.

9 The Dinner Party: How to Breathe Life into Literature

Chella Courington Livingston
Huntingdon College

As an undergraduate in the late sixties, I combed the library for likenesses of those remote authors I read in class. Whether Fitzgerald, Austen, or Pope, they were lifeless until I could give them flesh and blood, could make them concrete by digging up pictures and perusing biographies. How did they look? What did they wear? What was the gossip about them?

But there can be potential problems with the biographic approach to literature. One consideration is that we may confuse life and art, allowing a like or dislike of the author to shape our responses to the author's work. Woolf offers this caveat: "How far, we must ask ourselves, is a book influenced by its writer's life—how far is it safe to let the man interpret the writer? How far shall we resist or give way to the sympathies and antipathies that the man rouses in us . . .?" ([1932] 1986, 263). Another concern is that memoirs and biographies, diaries and letters, run the risk of presenting a personality that threatens to obliterate the artist altogether. Boswell's Johnson comes to mind: many of us recall the curmudgeon with his quips, yet few (except those whose specialty includes eighteenth-century literature) remember what Johnson actually wrote. A more recent victim of biography is Tennessee Williams, whose *Memoirs* tends to supersede his plays.

Despite the care with which a biographic approach must be taken, it can be very effective for generating interest in literature. Many of us are snoops by nature; we have an insatiable desire to pry into others' lives while trying to hide our own. Some 238 years ago Johnson remarked that biography appeals because it "enchain[s] the heart by irresistible interest" (1971, 94). Any list of bestsellers will confirm biography's enduring power to capture an audience.

Considering that biography made literature more accessible to me as an undergraduate, I have developed a role-playing project, called the Literary Dinner Party, for my undergraduate courses in literature. Dramatizing authors is not a new pedagogical concept; we have read about or experienced the professor who comes to class in the persona of Dickens or the students who assume authorial roles for class discussion. The novelty of my approach is its comprehensive nature. While the dinner party primarily encourages students to identify with authors and their work and to recreate some of the period's culture, the preparation also asks students to engage in other acts of a literary education: research, oral presentation, and expository writing that emphasizes creativity, voice, and audience. This project can be a relatively painless, even pleasurable, method for students to realize the objectives of most literature classes, with the main concern being to make literature more available. "This ain't such dry stuff after all," commented a physical education major after our Romantic dinner party.

Using my 1987–88 courses on Romantic and Victorian writers for reference, I will describe the twelve-week sequence of assignments leading up to the party. A successful project depends on timing—starting early in the term and pacing assignments. By the third week the instructor confers with all students about their chosen author. Though we are inclined to think that students with little background in the period require more guidance than others, this is often not the situation. All students, whether pre-med or English majors, need the instructor's expertise to help direct, as well as broaden, interests. For instance, an English major who had read a lot of Wordsworth's poetry asked if she could assume his persona. While agreeable, I asked her about the Romantic women writers. "They seem wimpy compared to the men," she returned, yet went on to say that she knew very little of the women's work. After reading Muriel Spark's *Mary Shelley* and delving into the *Grasmere Journals,* the student revised her opinion and focused on Dorothy Wordsworth for the dinner party. By the fourth week students settle on their writer.

Composing a biography is the next step. Assuming the author's voice and style, students write a first-person narrative based on the author's public and private life. This assignment involves them in a significant dialogue with the author, though students need not be deliberately conscious of this exchange. "Every human word implies not only the existence—at least in the imagination—of another to whom the word is uttered," writes Walter J. Ong, "but it also implies that the speaker has a kind of otherness within himself" (1962, 25).

When writing the first-person biography, the student writer's "otherness" is twofold: that of the authorial persona and of the student writer. This double perspective results in a kind of biography that felicitously combines fact and feeling. The student rendering of Elizabeth Barrett Browning's life begins: "It is at the window of Casa Guidi in our beloved Florence that I write this short 'history' of myself, believing that somewhere, someone will be interested in the story of the invalid Elizabeth who married a hero and truly did live happily ever after." Since the act of imitating voice and style contributes to the student's success in role-playing, the instructor spends class time showing how such imitations are made. Dickens and Eliot are ready models due to their distinctive authorial intrusions. Copies of each "writer's" biography are given to class members by the sixth week (midterm).

The third step consists of writing personal letters. Again in character, the student writes a one- to two-paragraph letter to each of the other authors. Such correspondence focuses on some aspect of the recipient's life or work that interests the sender. Along with the rhetorical emphasis on audience, this exercise gives students an opportunity to make creative use of their research. For example, the student pretending to be Wilde dates his letter to Elizabeth Barrett Browning, 1861—the year of her death, when Wilde was seven. Written in crayon with the handwriting, grammar, drawings, and voice fitting a seven-year-old, the letter reads: "Dear Mrs. Browning, You write lovely pomes. I wish i could write like you pomes. i am seven. How old are you?" The same student's letter to Swinburne, dated 1882, is founded in fact though the piece itself is fictitious. The Wilde persona not only refers to an actual letter by Swinburne, mocking Wilde, but also includes a classic Wildean epigram: "I have just been handed a letter written by you to Mr. E. D. Stedman. When those venomous lines were brought to my attention, I must say that I was gratified. 'There is only one thing worse than being talked about and that is not being talked about'." Students are expected to deliver their letters at least two weeks before the dinner since they provide the small talk. The letters can be used as occasional prompts during the evening, though guests ought to be able to talk without them.

Devising appropriate dress and preparing period food are the final steps. Relying on pictures of the author, students are asked to approximate a costume by rigging up whatever they can from their closets or those of sympathetic friends. One proviso: no money can be spent. The most original dress thus far has been that of the student impersonating Mary Ann Evans, alias George Eliot. Her right side was suitably male with a penciled mustache, boots, and knee pants;

her left was suitably female with sausage curls and a long petticoat and skirt.

When I first hosted these literary dinner parties, I fixed almost all the food, spending too much time over a stove while depriving students of yet another learning experience. Now I furnish period recipes from which students can select fairly easy dishes to prepare. By trial and error I have learned that dinner should come soon after the guests arrive, leaving about two hours for hopefully witty and literary conversation. Because the party takes the place of a final exam and counts 15 percent of the course grade, with the biographies and letters each weighing 15 percent, I remain in the background, evaluating costume, interest, and knowledge. Obviously, the project works more effectively in a group of ten to fifteen students. With larger classes, particularly survey courses of forty students, I divide them into smaller, discrete groups.

The key to a successful project is enthusiasm and enjoyment. Everyone should have fun. The idea is to attract students, to generate their interest in the study of literature—some of which, we must admit, has been taught in a dull, dry, and thoroughly stuffy manner. Our aim is to revitalize literature so that students will want to interact with it.

References

Johnson, Samuel. 1971. *The Rambler. Samuel Johnson: Rasselas, Poems, and Selected Prose.* 3d ed. Edited by Bertrand H. Bronson. New York: Holt, Rinehart, and Winston.

Ong, Walter J. 1962. *The Barbarian Within.* New York: Macmillan.

Woolf, Virginia. [1932] 1986. How Should One Read a Book? In *The Second Common Reader,* 258–70. San Diego: Harcourt Brace Jovanovich.

10 Portraying and Interpreting Literature through Art

Jill Hamilton
Deer Park High School
Cincinnati, Ohio

What started out as an unpretentious banner developed into an exciting and rewarding approach to teaching students how to interpret and portray literature while encouraging personal connections.

Each year the Cincinnati Public Library holds a banner contest. Any school—elementary, junior high, or high school—is welcome to submit a $4\frac{1}{2}' \times 10'$ fabric banner, hung by dowel rods, promoting either reading, libraries, or books. Entering this contest expanded the way I view and the way I teach literature.

Originally, I decided to enter the contest when my junior and senior high classes read their *first* novel. I thought the contest might help deter the possible apprehensiveness my below-average to average students might experience while engaging in their first novel.

In selecting books, I knew that the plot must be simple enough to understand and complex enough to question. I didn't consider how, or what, we would paint on our banner to promote the books. I thought that painting and entering the banner contest would simply be an "enrichment activity." Little did I realize that attempting, and ultimately succeeding, to guide the students in painting a picture reflecting the theme, elements, and depth of a story could be far more effective in connecting the students with literature than writing character analyses or answering comprehension question worksheets. My original goal was to select books that were enjoyable and understandable.

Before deciding on any books, I examined the profile of the students, their reading abilities, and their experience with analytical thinking skills. I have a unique advantage in determining my class characterization, because I am the only reading teacher in our junior/senior high. Because of the way our courses are scheduled, I almost always see students two years in a row, sometimes three years consecutively. (It should also be noted that I have no "assigned" novels in my course of study.)

I emphasize examining the class profile prior to selecting banner-designable books because interpreting and analyzing literature through art is very different than writing about literature. I discovered that teaching students to summarize a book in a picture rather than a paragraph required that I ask questions like, "What color could represent *sad?*" instead of "Think of a synonym for *sad.*" I had to ask, "What object could we incorporate in our banner that would represent several of the situations the main characters experienced?" rather than "Explain how this symbol fits in the story." And, although in some instances I received expected answers from the students, this type of question unpredictably sparked response from the reluctant readers as well as the proficient readers. It was when we began to paint that I observed different scenarios that reflected different thinking processes.

Some students had practiced and developed keen critical thinking skills. These students contributed many commendable, sometimes profound, ideas on how to portray the book. It was obvious that they were using all the techniques they had learned about analyzing literature. But it was the new awareness toward literature exhibited by hesitant readers that was particularly exciting. When these students shared their interpretation of the literature, they discovered that expressing themselves and their understanding of the work could be easier to draw than to write. Recognizing the class profiles and selecting books that would enhance the students' appreciation for literature, as well as improve their ability to understand and analyze literature, definitely lead to the success of the project.

I chose three books from different genres so that all my classes would be exposed to a variety of literature during the banner-making process. I knew we'd have to hang the banners from the ceiling while the paint on the fabric was drying, so the books would be on display during the project.

A nonfiction book about the Cincinnati Reds—*Baseball Cards of the Cincinnati Reds,* distributed by Topps at the baseball games—was appropriate for the seventh-grade class because I had not emphasized critical thinking skills as much as I had practiced basic comprehension skills with their basal texts. In addition, this was Cincinnati's bicentennial, and all the banners would be hung in the downtown public library.

Richard Peck's *Secrets of the Shopping Mall* (1980, Dell) was ideal for my eighth-grade "bi-level" class. Students would understand the basic plot that Barnie and Teresa, Peck's main characters, ran away from an undesirable home life and ended up living in a shopping mall. In addition to empathizing with Teresa and Barnie, students could also examine the possibility of an anarchic government, ruled by teenagers, existing within the mall.

On My Honor, by Marion Bauer (1987, Dell), is an eighty-page novel exposing the inner torment of a twelve-year-old boy after he witnesses his best friend drowning. This novel evokes an emotional and soul-searching response. The easy reading level is camouflaged by the complexity of the story. Since I was working with a high school class young in academic development, but of typical high school age, I felt it necessary to recognize students' maturity.

Because they were seemingly custom-designed for my classes, these three books, one nonfiction and two novels, encouraged the students to extend their analysis and inquiry beyond the basic plot. Because of the content, we discussed at length our own experiences in relation to the stories. Painting a picture reflecting the theme and content of the book only complemented students' involvement with the literature.

These are the objectives I wanted to accomplish during the course of the project:

1. promote a selected book
2. promote our reading class within the school
3. promote our school within the city
4. be proud of a long-term project
5. examine literature as a whole work, not as separate elements
6. create and design pictures
7. interpret and analyze literature without writing

Indeed, we met and achieved these objectives, but the real skills surfaced throughout the three weeks it took to complete our banners:

Teamwork. Immediately, we all learned that no one could have his or her way all the time. With fifteen to twenty students gathering around a ten-foot-long piece of fabric and deciding which idea best depicted the book's message, we learned to listen, think, and share ideas. It was interesting to witness the students defend their reasons for wanting "their" idea drawn on the banner. Students also pooled ideas in deciding how to cover up an accidental splash of paint by turning a mistake into an addition to the picture.

Different interpretations of literature. In discussing the literature, we discovered that often our own experiences help us to understand a character and his or her personality. After many discussions, we concluded that how one felt toward characters and their problems was a personal interpretation. As we were working on what could be compared to one giant oral book report, everyone realized that each individual can interpret a work differently. We discovered that the interpretation of literature doesn't necessarily seek one answer, but demands clarification. It was this exchange of understanding and collaborative learning that increased the students' perceptions of the novels.

Conclusion and speculation. I asked the students, during the designing stages and upon completion of the banners:

> Have we accurately depicted the complexity of the characters for our observers?
>
> Have we introduced all the dimensions of the plot?
>
> Have we convinced the viewer of this book's value?

I asked each class about the other classes' banners to see if the books were portrayed accurately. We had other teachers and administrators examine the banners and guess the plot and theme of our books. We were delighted to hear many "correct" interpretations along with some misdirected understandings. Where they could improve the banners, the students rethought their depictions and made adjustments in the picture. Listening and exchanging ideas with other teachers accented the point that interpretation of literature is a personal experience.

Understanding the book through details. For painting, we needed a foundation first, synonymous with a topic sentence. Once we determined what the main focus should be, we looked back through the literature to check on details such as "what color the bike was." The students came to understand that some details are included to "paint" a more vivid picture, not change the plot.

Analysis and inquiry beyond the basic story elements. It was through painting about literature that I fully understood how to present to the students what analyzing a story meant. "Analyze a story" implies much more than spitting back a plot sequence, as did summarizing an entire book in one picture. Because we were picturing both the plot sequence and the theme of the story in one glance, we were required to examine the novel in its entirety and summarize all components of the work in a picture, without words.

Pride. Each class had a different book to interpret. Over the course of the project, it was exciting to watch the classes "claim" their banner. As the year progressed I made, as did the students, allusions referring to "our banner and all that happened in the book."

We had grown to like and dislike each character we read about; it was as if we were trying to figure out what this character-turned-person did after the last chapter. I sensed a special pride in understanding a book so completely. This was the most fulfilling discovery that emerged upon the completion of our banners. While I taught the basic objectives, the truly significant skills transpired during the project.

Yes, coordinating regular reading and writing assignments with painting sessions was trying. Yes, we spilled paint in the radiator and had a fire drill when thirty feet of fabric covered with wet paint was on my floor, as well as on the hall floor. No, we didn't win the banner contest, nor will I relinquish character analyses or comprehension questions; but, yes, I will guide my students to interpret and portray literature through art again.

11 The Sophocles Connection

Mary Cobb
Western Washington University

Whenever I read Sophocles' *Antigone,* the play is about whatever is going on now. In the early 1970s, the proud rebel squared off against her ruler-uncle over Vietnam. In the middle seventies, Creon sounded like Nixon, invoking executive privilege in the name of national security. More recently, Creon's uneasy leadership lived again in a shaky substitute teacher who reportedly insisted that everyone in my senior humanities class move to the opposite side of the room, rather than believe he had my seating chart turned upside down.

I realize that high school students, young in experience, probably can't share fully my sense that Sophocles' tragedy is a multilayered portrait of the people we sometimes are and always have with us. Even so, I do want them to hear the words of Creon, Antigone, and the rest ring with relevance for their own lives, and I want them to discover that relevance for themselves. With this goal in mind, I recently prefaced in-class reading of the play with an activity to stimulate verbal clashes among my seniors over the very principles that troubled ancient Thebes. I hoped that the students would later recognize their own arguments in Sophocles' dialogue and feel some connections with the human drama twenty-five centuries old.

On the first day of the new unit, I said, "We all know that drama is conflict made visible and audible. Before we read some dramatic literature, we're going to consider some paired statements of ideals. Conflicts can arise when one person places greater emphasis on the first of the pair while another emphasizes the second. You will be a member of a group who will debate the *importance* of the statement assigned to you, when set against the ideal with which it is paired. Your job will be to supply arguments and examples from many different sources to convince us of the very great importance of your statement." Then I passed out the following paired statements, each a paraphrase or elaboration of dialogue in *Antigone:*

1a. People in authority should be consistent. If they have made rules, they should stick to them. Otherwise, the governed will have little confidence in their leaders' judgment.

1b. Good rulers yield when they know their course is wrong.

2a. Even though a law is unjust, it should be obeyed. Otherwise, there is a breakdown of law and order, and everyone suffers.

2b. Sometimes the only right thing to do is to break a bad law and publicly suffer the consequences.

3a. Death with honor is no better than death without honor: one person is going to be just as dead as the other. Life is the ultimate value.

3b. If people have no values they are willing to die for, their lives are not worth living.

4a. "To dream the impossible dream" is a nice thing to sing about, but it is foolish to take action against overwhelming odds.

4b. The Rodgers and Hammerstein song is right: "You've got to have a dream. If you don't have a dream, how're you going to make a dream come true?"

As a class, we brainstormed fruitful sources of examples and arguments that might be used for any of the eight statements—the students' own experiences; events in the news or from history and literature; hypothetical or real situations drawn from family life, work, school, sports, politics, friendships. Then, together, we quickly listed a few supporting arguments and examples for each statement within the last pair.

After some initial floundering to find support for *4a*, one student mentioned the appalling loss of life among idealistic young Muslims in the long seesaw of the Iran-Iraq war. Another spoke of high school athletes aiming for an unlikely professional sports career who foolishly spend all their time on athletics but neglect the disciplined study that could prepare them for more likely opportunities. One young artist remembered that, in Maugham's *Of Human Bondage* (on-going outside reading for the class), Fanny Price starves while squandering all her inept energy and resources in a futile attempt to become a great painter.

Defending *4b* was an easier task, since high school students are overwhelmingly idealistic. They talked about the way science fiction fantasies can be harbingers of scientific discoveries. They called up examples of Socrates and Martin Luther King and noted that social or political progress often moves forth over mutilated bodies.

After this preparation, I divided the class arbitrarily into six groups. Then, on a first-come, first-served basis, the groups selected from the remaining six statements the one they would defend. When late-choosers protested they agreed more strongly with their opponents' statement than their own, I reminded them that we had been able to support both the *4a* and *4b* statements, that each on the page was defensible, even if circumstances might call for an emphasis on one more than the other.

Although the paired statements are neither so specific nor so absolute in contrast as the affirmative and negative positions of a well-framed debate question, groups prepared their speaker or speakers for a presentation sequence similar to that in competitive debates, with a proponent of the *a* statement speaking first for two minutes, followed in order by a proponent of the *b* statement, then rebuttal from an *a* speaker, and finally rebuttal from the *b* group. Groups had ten minutes to prepare and to choose their speakers. Debates occurred on the same day, with the remaining class time divided equally among the three debates. As time allowed, class members could add additional arguments after each debate.

Debates were lively; participation, widespread; students, engaged and entertaining. The major problem with the lesson was that class time was too short for all ideas from the class to be expressed, much less fully explored.

Nevertheless, we began to read the play aloud on the following day, while the debates were fresh in our minds. Having already grappled with some of the conflicting attitudes of the Thebans, my students recognized their own arguments falling from their mouths again, but this time as the impassioned words of Sophocles' characters. When our resident Ismene read, "Impossible things should not be tried at all," I received a knowing smile from the contributor of our Fanny Price example. The *1b* rebuttal speaker couldn't resist a loud "All right!" at Teiresias' line, "Think: all men make mistakes,/ But a good man yields when he knows his course is wrong . . ." And so it went throughout our study of the play. Students quite naturally returned, in our discussions, to comment further on connections between the drama and their prereading debates.

I knew my plan was working when the students began to apply to their own time and circumstances the conflicts in the play that we had not already debated. When our stolid Creon told Teiresias, "Whatever you say, you will not change my mind," a classmate couldn't resist muttering, "*That's* my dad."

"It sounds like that substitute who made us all change seats," snorted another, for all to hear.

"It's *you,* yesterday!" boomed his crabby but accurate debate opponent.

I chuckled along with everyone else. Amazing and wonderful that Sophocles, so long ago and far away, knew my substitute—and my students—so well!

Reference

Sophocles. 1977. *Antigone.* In *The Oedipus Cycle,* translated by Dudley Fitts and Robert Fitzgerald. New York: Harcourt Brace Jovanovich.

12 Drama as a Way into Poetry

Elizabeth Komar
Vancouver, British Columbia, Canada

Educational drama is a valuable teaching tool within the English classroom for helping students of all ages and abilities reach a deeper understanding and appreciation of poetry. By lifting the printed word off the page, the dramatic process can bring life to the poem as well as give a fresh approach to routine teaching by providing a relevant context for writing and discussion.

Before reading Frances Cornford's poem, *Childhood,* I asked my ninth-grade students to recall any contact that they had had with elderly people. Many of the students shared their own personal experiences and observations concerning aging relatives or neighbors that ranged from humorous to poignant.

Students were then asked to consider old age from the perspective of a senior citizen. Each student, in role as an elderly person, shared at a meeting for senior citizens one aspect of old age that he or she did not like. By joining the role-playing as a social worker, I was able to elevate the tone and language of the students as well as give guidance and support to the participants. I was also able to help them sustain belief in their roles.

The students' responses revealed a wide range of concerns. Some were lonely as a result of the deaths of their friends, others felt a loss of independence due to their lack of mobility, and there were those who felt unattractive due to their wrinkles and varicose veins.

Students then chose a partner to work with. *A*s were to continue to be elderly people, while *B*s assumed the new role of a son or daughter of *A*. It was *B*'s difficult task to persuade *A* to move into a home for the aged. These improvised, five-minute discussions occurred concurrently throughout the classroom. The group discussion that followed these conversations revealed personal and cultural differences in caring for the aged, as well as students' concerns for providing alternate solutions.

The final preparation before the actual reading of the poem involved each student writing a letter as an elderly person to a son, daughter, or grandchild from the new residence. This gave students the opportunity to reflect upon their new insights and gave their writing a purpose.

One student wrote, "I have been here for over a month now and you said that I would settle in and I haven't. I may be old but I'm still strong and independent. I know I can't remember things as well or get around as easy as I used to."

Another student reflected, "Life in the home is depressing in some ways but it's better than being lonely and all by myself at home. I just wanted to know how you are and if you could visit me sometimes."

After reading the poem, the students were asked to write about their prereading experiences in their poetry response logs.

One student responded, "I found I could relate more to the poem after having to look at life from the perspective of someone who has an older, wiser, and totally different way of life."

Another student noted the unconventionality of the teaching style and commented that instead of the teacher posing questions, "*We* asked many questions."

Glimpses of family members were shared. "It made me think of my great grandmother who will be 96 years old this May who lives in a special apartment for older people. I think I'll write her a letter soon."

Another wrote, "It made me feel worried about what sort of things might happen to me when I get older. It made me feel sorry for my grandmother who is losing her memory and I fear that one day she might even forget me completely."

Anxiety about aging was revealed by one girl. "I can't imagine being old. Everybody says, 'Don't try to grow up too fast' but no one realizes that I want to be a teenager the rest of my life! I don't want to grow up. I love being young."

Drama can be helpful in enriching the learning process. It offers meaningful opportunities for both students and teachers to explore poetry and other forms of literature and their own personal responses to it.

13 Moral Dilemmas and *Death of a Salesman*

Eva Kafka Barron and David N. Sosland
Teaneck High School
Teaneck, New Jersey

In the age of television and VCRs, teaching literature and having students both enjoy and relate to it have become increasingly challenging tasks. Many of our students are cursory readers, hurrying to satisfy the number of pages assigned, without truly developing a relationship with the characters and voices of literature. TV soap operas with their stereotypical situations and pat solutions seem more real than the written word, and offer ready-made "value" systems which require little thought or input from young viewers.

Several approaches, however, have proven extremely successful in counteracting these problems and in bringing writing to life and relevance.

Death of a Salesman, Arthur Miller's timeless American drama, provides a high-powered means by which students can interact with literature. By implementing a variety of teaching methods, we have found that ninth- and tenth-grade students in particular can develop the ability to predict human reactions, analyze human behavior, and adapt the ideas in the literature to their own lives.

Before reading the actual text of *Death of a Salesman,* students receive a printed series of moral dilemmas based on specific situations in the play. These dilemmas might include the following:

1. John is captain of his high school football team. In fact, some fans say that he *is* the high school football team. First marking-period grades come out and John has failed math. According to school rules, any student who fails a major subject cannot participate on a school team. Without John the football team will lose its number one position. The coach approaches the math teacher and asks him to change John's grade. What should the teacher do?

2. Sixty-year-old Nathan has worked for the Rockleigh Company for thirty-five years. He has two years to go until he can retire. The Rockleigh Company no longer finds Nathan to be a contributing employee. In fact, he is being paid, but he is not helping the company. Should the boss fire Nathan?
3. Twenty-year-old Jason goes to the movies. While he leaves to get some popcorn, he spots his father sitting with his arm around a woman who is not Jason's mother. Later Jason's father denies that he even knew the woman. He wanted to see the movie, went in, sat down, felt cramped, and stretched out his arm. Jason does not believe his father. Should he tell his mother what he saw?
4. Sam is fifteen, and his brother Toby is thirteen. Sam, the first-born, is their father's favorite. In fact, Toby feels left out. The father does not see his favoritism, and therefore refuses to do anything about it. What should Toby do?
5. All through his school years, Bill's father had told Bill that he should study and get good grades because he had to go to law school and join the family firm. Bill gets accepted to a good law school, but after three months he realizes that this law career is not for him. His father will never forgive him if he does not join the law firm. What should Bill do?

Students discuss, in groups, possible options for and resolutions to these problems, and thus focus not only on their own value systems but discover a preview of the choices characters must confront in *Death of a Salesman.* (Be prepared for heated debates, both in small and, later, large groups!)

Another prereading activity designed to personalize and focus on one of the major themes in the play—the American dream—is the introduction of related poems, such as Langston Hughes's "Dream Deferred" and "Hold Fast to Dreams"; John Updike's "Ex-Basketball Player"; and "Lies" by Yevgeny Yevtushenko. These poems explore the frustration of postponed dreams, the importance of realistic goals rather than wishful thinking, the shattered dreams of unfulfilled potential, and the destructiveness that results from lying to oneself and others. Class discussion of these poems provides the key to understanding the false dreams that destroy the Loman family, and allows students to interact with specific ideas in the play.

After completing *Death of a Salesman,* students receive a series of options designed to broaden even further their insight into the complex relationships within any family. These options include the following:

1. The moral dilemmas, presented as a prereading activity, are reexamined in the light of the Lomans' situation. This follow-up discussion serves as an excellent values-clarification exercise.
2. Students are helped to develop greater empathy toward the characters by actually pretending to become a character of their choice via the introductory phrase, "Hello, my name is . . ." Done as an oral presentation or an informal essay, this assignment asks students to examine how their individual characters feel about themselves and others; how they see others affecting them; what their dreams and goals are; what frustrations they encounter, and what attempts they make to solve them.
3. Yet another activity for helping students extend their analysis of the play by relating specific situations to their own lives is the creation of a fictional "diary." Here are some suggested topics provided by the teacher:
   - Like Willie Loman, I once used lies or excuses to escape an uncomfortable situation. Here's what happened . . .
   - My brother/sister seems to be my parents' favorite. Here's how I deal with the situation . . .
   - I think the things that make a person popular and well-liked are . . .
   - My parents' expectations of me don't always match my own. Let me explain . . .
   - Other than money, the things that would make me happy in life are . . .

Students enjoy responding privately to these sample "entries" in booklet form, and once again they gain expanded insight into both the play and themselves.

We have found that students of *all* abilities and backgrounds are able to interact more intensely with the literature when these activities are provided; and although they have been designed for *Death of a Salesman,* they can be adapted to any other literary work for a variety of grade levels.

II The Reading and Writing Connection with Literature

14 The Reader's Work: Learning through Enactment

Richard Jenseth
Pacific Lutheran University

In the opening lines of *Textual Power* (1985), Robert Scholes talks about a "dialogue between teaching and theory" which flows through his book. The focus of this dialogue is the impact of theory on classroom teaching and, interestingly enough, the impact of teaching on theory. In some sense, this essay is an extension or a continuation of that dialogue. I will describe a sequence of writing and reading assignments that uses John Hersey's *Hiroshima* to engage the critical imaginations of my composition students, and I will suggest something of the theory that has shaped, and has been shaped by, the sequence.

In the broadest sense, this activity attempts to introduce students to questions about the nature of interpretation, understanding, and composing by asking them to engage in these activities and then to reflect on the consequences of what they have done. In other words, the heart of this sequence is "learning through enactment": we don't study interpretation and composing but participate in them, then use what we have learned to learn more. Our efforts to learn from experience and critical reflection are unified by the design of the activity—a "cumulative" or "spiraling" sequence—that is, a series of interrelated assignments, each of which assumes the last and anticipates the next.

Finally, while the sequence lends intellectual and pedagogical coherence to the course, the use of a single, whole text addresses my concern about the quality of the reading experience in my composition classes. I chose to put *Hiroshima* at the center of things because it asks us to confront difficult social and political issues, and because of its power and terrifying beauty. But I also chose Hersey's book because it's a *book.* Frankly, I had grown frustrated with prepackaged

An earlier version of this chapter appeared in the Staffroom Interchange section of *College Composition and Communication* (May 1989; 40 [2]: 215–19) under the title, "Understanding *Hiroshima:* An Assignment Sequence for Freshman English."

commercial readers, or at least with making the three- or four-page essay (or excerpt) the focus of critical reading. I believe reading and understanding a whole text challenges students in a way a brief essay (or collection of brief essays) cannot. Readers live with a book differently; they see reading differently, and themselves as readers. Certainly, extended work with a whole text demands (and rewards) a different kind of patience and persistence, especially as part of a sequence built around sustained, tough-minded *rereading*.

The practice of rereading is another important pedagogical premise of this sequence: fewer assigned readings, but a more rigorous reading of what is read. Roland Barthes calls rereading an act "contrary to the commercial and ideological habits of our society, which would have us 'throw away' [the reading] once it has been consumed so that we can move on to another" (1974, 15). For Barthes, a single reading of a text limits readers to what they already know how to see; rereading returns them to the text with a critical eye, probing, questioning, looking from various perspectives in order to get beyond the "already read." *Hiroshima* works well for such a sequence because its size (fewer than 100 pages) and accessibility make extended rereading feasible, while its power and complexity reward sustained analysis. Other likely choices would be Terkel's *Working,* McPhee's *Coming into the Country,* and *The Autobiography of Malcolm X,* all fairly long but easily adaptable. I have also used Cabeza de Vaca's *Adventures in the Unknown Interior of America,* the bizarre and riveting journal of a sixteenth-century Spanish explorer lost eight years in the wilderness of the New World.

This particular sequence (see Figure 1) is an eight- or nine-week activity, the center of which is our determined rereading of *Hiroshima.* Before we get to Hersey's text, however, the first four assignments get us thinking about our own daily experiences with observing, interpreting, and composing. Assignment 1 begins with writing from experience, a reflective essay about a job which, for whatever reason, was or was not right for students at that time in their lives. It is important that this task requires more than venting emotion or a simple listing of duties. As writers recount the experience, they must weigh events in the larger context of their lives; in a sense, they must interpret the text of their own experience. In our workshop of early drafts we begin to address important interpretive issues, especially the importance of perspective and context, and we begin to take seriously the quality of our composing—its usefulness to the writer as well as to the reader.

Assignment 1	*Work, Work, Work* A descriptive narrative about a work experience.
Assignment 2	*"All the News . . ."* An analysis of news media reporting of events.
Assignment 3	*Looking, Seeing, Reporting* Our efforts to produce "objective" descriptions.
Assignment 4	*Rereading Assignment 1*
Assignment 5	*Prereading of* Hiroshima *(in-class)*
Assignment 6	*Interview: War and Memory* Interview someone who lived during the war—report on what they say about Hiroshima.
Assignment 7	*Reading Journal* (in response to each chapter)
Assignment 8	*"Just the Facts"* In-class writing about Hersey's use of "facts."
Assignment 9	*Shelving* Hiroshima Our efforts to re-see the text in terms of familiar genres.
Assignment 10	*Reread Assignment 9*
Assignment 11	Hiroshima: *1946/1990: A Review Essay*
Assignment 12	*Telling Lives: A Biographical Essay* Weighing, selecting, shaping details to produce a portrait of a "life."

Figure 1. Sequence for studying John Hersey's *Hiroshima*

In Assignment 2, we look at how professional journalists observe and report events. For several days we analyze newspapers, magazines, and television news to see how these "factual accounts" give us the world in words and pictures. We look closely at the conventions of reporting: layout and design (why all those clicking typewriters behind Peter Jennings?), the language of headlines, how "news" is distinguished from "analysis" or "editorializing." Fairly quickly the issue of bias or slanting comes up, but rather than debate the relative fairness of particular media or reporters, we examine the idea of slanting itself: What does it mean to slant the telling of an event? Is it always intentional? What would ideal, purely objective "news" be like?

We quickly test our theories with Assignment 3, "Looking, Seeing, Reporting." Students are sent out to describe a single place, capturing the look and feel of the place as accurately and vividly as they can. The assignment warns them: "Be accurate, clear, objective; be colorful, vivid, even entertaining . . . that's what we expect of good reporters, no?" In small workgroups later in our class workshop, we marvel at how different observers saw a single place so differently, and we playfully expose even the slightest hints of bias, including the subtle slanting of word choice and selective detail. As a follow-up, Assignment 4 asks students to reread what they wrote for Assignment 1. In small groups in class they work to interpret their interpretations, paying particular attention to how they had created themselves, how they had situated themselves with events and other people. Through such critical self-reflection, revision becomes much more than polishing prose: it is a serious experimenting with language, and thereby an experimenting in ways of seeing and understanding.

Then we move to *Hiroshima,* Hersey's brilliant telling of events on August 6, 1945. Through a five- or six-week process of reading, interpretation, and criticism, we will work towards an understanding of the text and of the event it reports. We begin with several "prereading" activities (see Cooper and Axlerod 1987). For example, we examine the book itself—the picture of the familiar atomic mushroom on its cover, the blurb on the back cover that calls *Hiroshima* a "journalistic masterpiece" and "the true story" of the "greatest single man-made disaster in history." Then we begin to explore the larger social and historical context in which we read, and that in which Hersey wrote. As David Hoy puts the problem, understanding a text involves clarifying not just its "internal features" but also "the interpreter's input," including, says Hoy, "the tradition in which the interpreter stands" (1978, 52). In other words, reading is never an "innocent encounter" with a text. Understanding *Hiroshima* will require both "close reading" and critical self-awareness of *our* own situation—cultural, social, political. What presumptions, prejudices, and experiences do we bring to the activity of making meaning? As Robert Scholes reminds us, "In order to teach the interpretation of a literary text, we must be prepared to teach the cultural text as well" (1985, 33).

This reflection on the cultural text begins by fleshing out the tacitly acquired "story" our culture has already told us about Hiroshima. What do we already know or think we know about this event? Assignment 5 has us list every fact, myth, and suspicion we can recall about the bomb and the war. At first, these eighteen-year-olds plead ignorance, and though it is true that no one person knows much, our collective knowledge is impressive: the name of the plane, the size of the bomb, the story of its creation, the story of the decision to use the bomb. Others recall bits of geopolitical speculation, picked up in history class or from relatives: we *really* dropped the bomb in order to impress the Russians; we didn't warn the Japanese because we wanted to test the bomb on living subjects.

Then we consider the history of this text—that it was written and first read in 1946, soon after the war, when Americans knew little about the bomb and felt quite differently about the Japanese. Can we ever read that *Hiroshima?* Even those who have not seen a John Wayne war film are familiar with the commonplace images they exploited: the "sneaky Jap," cruel, godless, fanatical. We briefly sketch out our own social representations of Japan and the Japanese, and of our current "enemy," the Russians (who, interestingly enough, are also represented as devious, godless, and fanatical). Finally, we consider our own nuclear predicament, our own lives with the bomb—invisible, yet always present. We talk about how through movies like *The Day After* or *Testament* we already know what death at ground zero must look like.

This "continual mediation of past and present," which David Hoy calls "a condition for the very possibility of interpretation" (1978, 52), continues throughout the sequence. Assignment 6, for example, asks students to interview a relative or family friend who was alive during the war to see what they recall feeling about Hiroshima. What we learn from this task helps us piece together the logic of the act: revenge for Pearl Harbor, a quick end to the war. But we also learn from *doing* the task: students experience the difficulties of accurately transcribing, interpreting, and reporting firsthand accounts, an important source for Hersey's depiction of events.

Finally comes our first collaborative reading of the book. It is fewer than 100 pages long, so we read it quickly, using class time to discuss the reactions and questions that students recorded in a reading journal (Assignment 7). Near the end of this week of reading and discussion, Assignment 8 asks them to observe and list the kinds of "facts" Hersey selects to tell his version of Hiroshima. It is a fascinating combination of impassively stated historical and scientific facts—the temperature at ground zero was 6,000 degrees Celsius (about the temperature of the surface of the sun)—and intimate personal facts about the survivors—Dr. Fujii had been restless and depressed the days before the blast; as Mr. Tanimoto carried slimy living bodies to safety after the explosion, he had to keep telling himself "These are human beings, these are human beings."

Our fussing with facts and sources of information continues over the next three weeks as we reread Hiroshima in light of other factual accounts: traditional history, official army reports, other firsthand accounts by journalists (Richard Rhodes's *The Making of the Atomic Bomb;* and Edwin Fogelman's *Hiroshima: The Decision to Use the A-Bomb).* We also watch a propaganda film that combines excerpts from Hersey's book with terrifying footage of horribly wounded children and a devastated landscape. Our discussion focuses on the differences and similarities between these versions of Hiroshima, particularly the way facts are selected and organized. What gets highlighted? What gets left out? What are the sources of their facts? Again, Hersey was not a witness to the blast, so most of what he tells comes from what ethnographers call "received stories," Hersey selecting from and shaping the already selected perceptions of his six informants. What claim does his text make (implicitly or explicitly) to the "truth" of Hiroshima? What sort of authority should it claim? How are we to evaluate such claims?

With Assignment 9 we spend a week or more rereading this text in terms of conventional and very convenient generic categories. The assignment has students working in an imaginary library with only four shelves: history, journalism, propaganda, fiction. They must decide where to place a single copy of Hiroshima, and they must defend their choice with supporting examples from the text. Obviously, the first challenge is to define the four categories, but as we puzzle over definitions, we also puzzle over the source of their authority: Who says what history is? Or propaganda? Then we reexamine how this text behaves, and how we behave towards it. Certainly what happened on August 6, 1945, was an important historical event, but can a text so rich with intimate personal details of ordinary individuals be "history"? Beyond doubt, the blast and the terrible suffering are more than the product of Hersey's imagination; but what are we to make of this text's "fictional" qualities: its elaborate characterization, its complex narrative pattern, its subtle but persistent use of figurative language?

And what of the book's stance towards the reader? Despite its reassuring third-person omniscient voice (a voice we recognize from our analysis of journalism), most students are suspicious of this book and of Hersey's intentions. Hersey seldom overtly intrudes in the narrative, yet somehow the writing feels intensely personal, passionate. Artful trickery, or is the passion somehow in us? All along readers have felt bullied by the unrelenting cadence of detail: skin slipping from limbs "in huge glove-like pieces," melted eyes running down faces, frightened children asking "Why is the sky so dark? Why did our house fall down?" Is Hersey a calculating propagandist or an innocent messenger? Is the terror in the text, or is it somehow rooted in our own perilous situation?

After several more weeks of rereading and discussion, Assignment 10 asks them to reread and reconsider their genre choices. After heated class discussion, some stand pat while others change their choices, or at least revise their rationale. Of course, the aim of all this fussing is not right or wrong answers but better and better questions. Certainly, there are differences between history and fiction, or journalism and propaganda, but what is the nature of these differences? On what basis do we "authorize" certain ways of depicting events as true, or at least more true than others?

Assignment 11 comes near the end of our work with *Hiroshima;* students are asked to compose and prepare for publication a review-essay, written for peers, to be published in the campus newspaper. We have worried this text from multiple angles of vision, but as the philosopher Nelson Goodman remarks, "Awareness of varied ways of seeing paints no pictures" (1978, 21). It's time to paint pictures, time to articulate a critical stance towards this book and what it does. What will this book demand of readers? Is it worth reading—why or why not? This exercise in critical practice is a complex social act: speaking to and "on behalf of" a group of which the writer is a member (Scholes 1985, 25), and rereading the text for an audience who (like us eight weeks earlier) knows little of the event and nothing of the book.

In the final week of the sequence, Assignment 12 returns us to the personal narrative, to the stories that constitute our own lives and selves. Students are to compose a biographical narrative about a close friend or relative. In a sense they are asked to compose a life, but throughout this sequence, in our analysis of texts, in reflecting on our own composing, we come to see that *all* texts—including our own—are never transparent, unmediated records of events or neutral collections of facts. These writers can't give us the whole truth of a life any more than Hersey could offer *the* truth of Hiroshima. There's no single, univocal truth to be had, and even if there were, as Nelson Goodman points out, the whole truth would be paralyzing: "too vast, variable, clogged with trivia" (1978, 19). These writers will have to do what Hersey has done, what all journalists or historians must do: sort through an infinitely complex reality, selecting from and shaping received stories, historical facts, personal impressions. In the end, the quality of their compositions is judged by their usefulness, by what

Goodman calls "their relevance and their revelations, their force and their fit—in sum, their *rightness*" (1978, 19).

The sequence concludes with several days of consolidation and reflection. Students organize everything they have written into a project portfolio. Before they turn it in for my evaluation, I ask that they review and evaluate their own work and their contributions to the larger enterprise. I share with them my sense of our work together, then I open the discussion to comments and questions about what we have seen and done and what we think it means to us. For my part, I believe students understand texts in a new way, and reading, and themselves as readers. As we talk one last time about our own nuclear predicament, a world in which more and bigger weapons are said to make us safer, my hope is that they look at this world differently, with what Vincent Leitch (1985) calls "a vigilance about language" and "active suspicion" about how that world presents itself to us: as natural, inevitable, unalterable.

References

Barthes, Roland. 1974. *S/Z.* New York: Hill and Wang.

Cooper, Charles R., and Rise B. Axlerod. 1987. *Reading Critically, Writing Well.* New York: St. Martin's.

Fogelman, Edwin. 1964. *Hiroshima: The Decision to Use the A-Bomb.* New York: Scribner's.

Goodman, Nelson. 1978. *Ways of Worldmaking.* Indianapolis: Hackett Publishing.

Hersey, John. 1946. *Hiroshima.* New York: Knopf.

Hoy, David. 1978. *The Critical Circle.* Berkeley: University of California Press.

Leitch, Vincent B. 1985. Deconstruction and Pedagogy. In *Writing and Reading Differently,* edited by G. Douglas Atkins and Michael L. Johnson, 16–26. Lawrence, Kansas: University Press of Kansas.

Rhodes, Richard. 1986. *The Making of the Atomic Bomb.* New York: Simon and Shuster.

Scholes, Robert. 1985. *Textual Power.* New Haven: Yale University Press.

15 Ambiguous Texts in Teaching the Reading of Literature

Miriam B. Mandel
Tel Aviv University

Why is it, we have all wondered at some point, that so many of our students are so tentative, so ill at ease in their approach to literature? They have had years of English classes and a number of English teachers; they have been exposed to scores of poems and stories. Why, then, are they so reluctant to speak about literature and why, when they do speak, are their answers so limited and, sometimes, so inappropriate?

The oft-heard student complaint, "I don't know what the teacher wants," should, I am convinced, be taken seriously. It reveals neither ignorance nor disinterest, but a degree of sophistication, an awareness that literature contains many possibilities, any number of things that might be "wanted." By the time they reach college, most students know from their own classroom experiences that personal history and ideologies affect the reading of texts, so that different readers construct different readings and different interpretations of the same text. They also know that the text itself is not always straightforward: irony, under- and overstatement, a complicated or shifting narrative technique may cloud the issue.

Even a basic question, like "Who is the protagonist of the story?" cannot always be answered easily or unambiguously. *The Great Gatsby,* as Wayne Booth points out, "can be described as either Nick [Carraway]'s experience of Gatsby or as Gatsby's life as seen by Nick" (1961, 346), and the student cannot possibly know in which direction the teacher is headed, or if perhaps the teacher is headed in both directions at the same time. Cleanth Brooks and Robert Penn Warren (1959) see Nick Adams as the main character of Hemingway's short story "The Killers"; Ronald Crane (1967) argues vigorously that Nick is not the main character, but merely a device to facilitate narration.

When we ask our students to respond to a text, then, we should not be surprised that they retreat into silence or into plot summary. They might, of course, not have any answers to our questions. But I think it more likely that they have an answer but not the confidence that the answer will be appropriate—or even acceptable. Even with the tolerance taught us by reader-response theories, we are all well aware "that we can misread, and that some readings are better than others" (Laff 1984, 494).

How can we alleviate our students' discomfort? How can we help our students become responsive and confident readers (see Bergstrom 1983; Newkirk 1984; Hunt 1982)? Clearly, we cannot take complexity out of literature; reading is and must be a complex issue. But we *can* help our students; by asking more limited, more precise, more text-oriented questions, we can show them *where* the answers come from. A closer acquaintance with the text will give students not only the facts but also the confidence that they need before venturing an opinion or an interpretation.

When I first taught Hemingway's short story "The Killers" a number of years ago, I used the then-standard approach: the students read the story at home and came to class to discuss it. When I asked what the story might be about, I of course got plot summary: "The story is about two men who come into a lunchroom looking for a Swedish fellow whom they want to kill." When I pressed, I got the usual variety of silences and a few tentative suggestions (the dark side of humanity? crime? death?) and one or two "socially-aware" guesses: the story is about prejudice (because Sam is "the nigger") or about homosexuality (because the killers say that George will make someone a fine wife). When I mentioned Brooks and Warren's phrase "the discovery of evil" (1959) and told my students about rites of passage and initiation into manhood, the phrases were dutifully written into notebooks, but from their expressions I could tell that the students saw very little connection between these ideas and the tension-packed but inconclusive story they had just read. They may have learned how these critics read the story, but they had not learned anything about the reading of stories.

The next time I assigned the story, I had the students spend a class meeting simply establishing the facts of the story. Basing my technique on Laurence Perrine's "General Questions for Analysis and Evaluation" (1959, 367–69), I asked very specific questions about place (Where does the story take place? How many different settings are there? Is any setting used more than once? Where is everyone standing or sitting?) and time (When does the story take place? In what year, at what time of year, at what time of day?). It soon emerged that, although they had obviously read the story, the students couldn't answer many of these questions. What was most interesting to me was their failure to recognize these as questions of *fact,* the unambiguous answers to which are available in the text. They responded to these specific questions with the same silences and the same tentative guesswork that the more general and potentially loaded questions, like "What is the story about?" had elicited. And they looked at me, instead of at the text, to see if their suggestions had hit the mark. Eventually answers emerged, both wrong answers (it's deep winter, because the killers are wearing coats and gloves) and right answers (the story takes place in late fall, in the late afternoon and early evening). And as I insisted on evidence from the story to support their answers, more and more students began to look at their books instead of at me.

After the facts of time and place were established, we moved on to the facts about the characters. As if we were filling out a questionnaire, we identified first name, last name, age, martial status, employment, ethnic background, and educational level as best we could (see Wresch 1983). We noted where the story offered precise detail and where it didn't: the students realized that they could describe not only the faces and clothes, but also the motivation and effectiveness of the killers in more detail than those of any other characters in the story. The killers' coats and gloves, for example, which had earlier been seen as insignificant (providing protection from the weather) or misleading (it must be winter), now were seen as functional and important: the coats hid guns and the gloves prevented fingerprints, thus supplying evidence for the professionalism of the killers. About Ole, however, they could only say that he was a boxer and of Swedish parents (very tall and maybe blond). Several students suggested that he had somehow done something wrong, for which he deserved to be killed, but by now my constant insistence, "How do you know? What in the story tells you this?" led them to drop these guesses as untenable. Because the questions were specific and the answers obtainable from the text, the students became more and more willing to talk, to produce answers, and more importantly, to defend them. They were able to establish some matters with certainty (that the killers were cold, well-trained, and well-equipped professionals; that Ole, Sam, and George immediately recognized them for what they were; that Nick did not) and some with near-certainty (that the killers would eventually return and kill Ole, that they did not worry about the police, that Nick is younger and less experienced than the others). This time, I didn't even get to ask, "And what do you think that the story as a whole is about?" The students talked easily about growing up, learning about life, realizing that evil can't be evaded. To this class, as opposed to my earlier one, the concepts of initiation, rites of passage, loss of innocence, and the inescapability of evil came naturally. Brooks and Warren's sophisticated thesis that "the story is about the discovery of evil" was not, to them, a "far-out" interpretation, capriciously imposed upon the text in some esoteric way that only a teacher, and not a student, could manage. The point is not that they all accepted this one reading as "correct," but that they saw where it came from.

D. H. Lawrence encouraged us to "trust the tale," and indeed the story itself is a wonderful teacher, if we will only look closely enough. If students have the text well enough in hand, they will be aware of complexity without being made nervous by it, and less likely to rely on an outside authority for an interpretation. They will see interpretation of literature as a self-sponsored instead of a school-sponsored activity (Huff 1983).

How can we help our students acquire the tools and the confidence that will enable them to interact profitably with literature, and how can we do this within the limited time we spend together? My answer to the first question is to deal with texts more intensively; my answer to the second is to deal with fewer texts but to choose them very carefully. I believe that the most complex and sophisticated text is the most efficient, because it allows students to explore a maximum number of possibilities while staying within the same text and the same facts. A Shakespearean problem play or a Jamesian novel would, of course, be the ideal text because of the complexity, the suggestiveness, the ambiguities, the many layers of meaning that offer themselves for unraveling. But high school students (and most college freshmen) will respond more easily to a shorter text, one that is easily accessible and yet offers many possibilities for interpretation. So-called "flawed," "ambiguous," or "problematic" stories are the most rewarding and most efficient teaching tools for our purpose; although relatively short, they are rich in possibilities.

A story that contains an internal inconsistency or contradiction opens itself to many variant readings, in contrast to a more closely perfect work of art, which limits the possibilities of interpretation. Hemingway's great story, "The Killers," for example, allows a number of interpretations, but it excludes others. While we can argue that the story is about evil (the discovery of evil, the variety of responses to evil, the effects of evil), we cannot relate that evil to virtue: virtue is irrelevant to the story. We can discuss the attempt to escape or evade evil, but we cannot talk of triumphing over or defeating evil—the story will not allow it.

Wayne Booth (1961) has identified several other ambiguous or flawed stories, among them Henry James's "The Aspern Papers," Sherwood Anderson's "I Want to Know Why," and William Faulkner's "That Evening Sun." Any of these texts would, I think, help us teach our students to become responsive, responsible, and confident readers in the short time we have with them.

Our students are, generally speaking, naive enough to read superficially but sophisticated enough to sense that modern questions about literature lead to complex answers. Both their inexperience and their sophistication work to make them uncomfortable. Aware that complex readings are required but unable to provide them, students tend to rely on the teacher instead of on themselves or on the text for an understanding of literature. When the teacher removes herself or himself (by asking that the student provide the interpretation) or is removed (the student having finished the course), the student is in trouble.

Our job, then, is not to teach this or that reading of a story, but to teach students to read the story by and with themselves. In Haas and Flower's terms, we need "to move from merely *teaching texts* to *teaching readers*" (1988, 169). The "solution" I have proposed is the very basic one of showing students how to come to grips with the facts of the text, of helping them assume control of the text. With an "ambiguous" or "problematic" text, students have to work harder both to determine what happens in the story and to decide which of the possibilities they are going to accept. Such an ambiguous story, then, is a highly efficient way for us to provide our students, through one text, with the tools that will enable them to deal independently, skillfully, and therefore confidently with the issues of literature in many other texts.

References

Bergstrom, Robert F. 1983. Discovery of Meaning: Development of Formal Thought in the Teaching of Literature. *College English* 45 (8): 745–55.

Booth, Wayne. 1961. *The Rhetoric of Fiction.* Chicago: University of Chicago Press.

Brooks, Cleanth, and Robert Penn Warren. 1959. Interpretation. In *Understanding Fiction,* 2d ed., edited by Cleanth Brooks and Robert Penn Warren, 303–12. New York: Appleton-Century-Crofts.

Crane, Ronald S. 1967. Ernest Hemingway: "The Killers." In *The Idea of the Humanities and Other Essays, Critical and Historical,* 303–14. Chicago: University of Chicago Press.

Haas, Christina, and Linda Flower. 1988. Rhetorical Reading Strategies and the Construction of Meaning. *College Composition and Communication* 39 (2): 167–83.

Huff, Roland K. 1983. Teaching Revision: A Model of the Drafting Process. *College English* 45 (8): 800–16.

Hunt, Russell A. 1982. Toward a Process-Intervention Model in Literature Teaching. *College English* 44 (4): 345–57.

Laff, Ned Scott. 1984. Review: Teaching the Text in Class. *College English* 46 (5): 493–502.

Newkirk, Thomas. 1984. Looking for Trouble: A Way to Unmask Our Readings. *College English* 46 (8): 756–66.

Perrine, Laurence. 1959. *Story and Structure.* New York: Harcourt, Brace and World.

Wresch, William. 1983. Computers and Composition Instruction: An Update. *College English* 45 (8): 794–99.

16 Students and Literature: Intimate Friends

Maureen H. A. Morrissey
Hollinger Elementary School
Tucson, Arizona

Perched on a stool in front of my class, I display the front cover of a picture book. A buzz rises in the room as the students guess what the book will be about; some read the title and the author's name, while others examine the cover picture. I call on several students to share their predictions aloud. Dramatically, I open the book, read aloud the first page, and show the picture to the class. Amidst whispers of "I want that one," and "not me," I replace the book on the chalkboard tray and reach for another one of the twenty books displayed there; it is in Spanish. The whole action takes about one minute.

This is the first day of my year-long literature studies program, using books as a take-off point of study in a seven-day cycle. With books, I can guide growth in reading ability, help students to build values, provide vicarious learning situations, and provide pleasurable and informative experiences. The source of the books itself becomes a lesson: library books make the library important, books from home make home and the student feel important. My literature studies program encompasses a great deal of reading fundamentals. Children are motivated and turned on. They read for a variety of reasons, including pleasure, information, curiosity, and challenge. Students delve deeper into the meaning of literature and literature gets deeper inside the minds and hearts of students. The variety of literature available means that each student, regardless of background, will find suitable reading material.

The program is based on a seven-day schedule during which students choose a book and a partner, read the chosen book, rotate to five enrichment centers, and finally, share with the whole class an evaluation of the overall experience. At the end of the seven days, we choose other books and begin again. I originally prepared this model for a third-grade bilingual class of English- and Spanish-speaking students in Tucson, Arizona, that showed a need for teacher-run structure or centers with constant reassurance and teacher guidance. It is preferably a transition or introduction to a more student-centered or student-run program. This group of students was given several important but limited choices to make within the structure, with the objective of helping them become accustomed to making and following through on choices. Twenty picture books from our school library were displayed so that the children could see the covers; the books, in English and Spanish, ranged in difficulty from simple patterns (*¿Dónde está Spot?*) to story books with complicated plots (*Jumanji*). During the introduction of the books, I showed the print to the students so they got an idea of the level of difficulty.

Once books are introduced, students choose partners. Each pair is given a numbered card and is called up in numerical order to choose one of the books. Then the pair goes off to read together. Each student carries along a folder of construction paper. Stapled to the folder is a sheet of paper on which students record their partner, date, and chosen book. There is a section for the teacher to write a grade or comments on the child's experience with the chosen book. The folder also has a pocket stapled on it, in which students keep works-in-progress related to the books. The first day's lesson, from introduction to reading, takes approximately an hour.

For the next five days, three teacher-assigned pairs become a group that rotates to five centers, each stop lasting approximately forty minutes. The class helps decide where in the room to place each center. One center has students evaluate their books as to plot development, characters, and setting on a "summary sheet" (Figure 1). Students refer back to the book in order to come to agreement about which characters were most important and what the crisis of the plot was. There is a section on the summary sheet where students write down words they did not know. We review these later, using context clues to figure them out.

A second center uses writing to extend students' experience with reading. The assignments for writing in this case were teacher-chosen and included: Write Part 2 of your book or rewrite your book from the point of view of one of the characters. The assignments gave these students enough freedom to feel ownership of their work, while at the same time providing the structure so many of them required. The students' work from this center varied from little risk-taking to wildly creative, with many students moving forward along this continuum through the year.

Title____________________

Pages____________________

Author____________________

This story was____________________

Setting (Where did the story take place?)____________________

____

Main characters (Their names and a sentence about why they are important.)

1. ____________________

____

2. ____________________

____

3. ____________________

____

<u>Main Events</u>

1. How did it begin?____________________

____

____

2. What was the problem?____________________

____

____

3. How was the problem solved? How did the story end?____________________

____

____

____

New words I came across: 1. ____________________

2. ____________________ 3. ____________________

4. ____________________ 5. ____________________

Figure 1. Story summary sheet

At a third center, students create artwork pertaining to their chosen books. We often vary the materials, size of the artwork, and the art medium. Again, this group produced a wide range of creative work. Interestingly, those who were more creative in writing were not necessarily creative in art. A fourth center has students creating games or puzzles based on their books. A favorite of our class was word-search making in which each child made a word-search using characters' names, adjectives, nouns, antonyms, etc. from their chosen books (Figure 2). These were placed in a basket and students who found time during the remainder of the day could choose to search for the words. Other game ideas use sentence strips or word cards. Students could create a jigsaw puzzle by drawing and writing on a sturdy paper that will then be cut to make puzzle pieces and can be solved by another student.

The fifth center is a reading strategy lesson in which the teacher works with the group on a teacher-chosen strategy lesson. These lessons arise from the teacher's awareness of needed reading strategies and may include grammar, phonics, or comprehension strategies. For example, I noticed that many students were not able to identify a central problem in a story. Using Yetta Goodman and Carolyn Burke's *Reading Strategies: Focus on Comprehension* (1980), I worked with each group on this important strategy. We read a story together, stopping often to predict the next part. We looked for the problem that needed solving in the story. It is important to accept and discuss all of the students' responses during such a lesson. In this way, students will feel comfortable sharing ideas and predictions. This particular lesson can be given more than once throughout the year.

On the seventh day of the cycle the whole class shares and discusses work from their folders, displays and explains art projects, and discusses the books (informal book reporting). I also like to report on and build on "discoveries" made in strategy lesson groups. In each cycle, I grade and comment on the students' experiences based on their work in the folder, their choice of book, and their sharing on Day 7, during which I jot down notes on students' contributions to the discussion.

Our class enjoyed the literature studies program because students became intimate friends with books and with written language. They learned to take risks, to accept challenges, and to not fear failure. Without exception every student improved in reading ability as well as in self-confidence and in eagerness to read. These improvements spread to all other subjects, most especially writing. This program

Create a puzzle using 20 words that you find in your story. List all 20 words below the puzzle. Fill in the blank spaces that are left with other letters so that the words you hid will be harder to find.
Look for Words That Are ______________________________

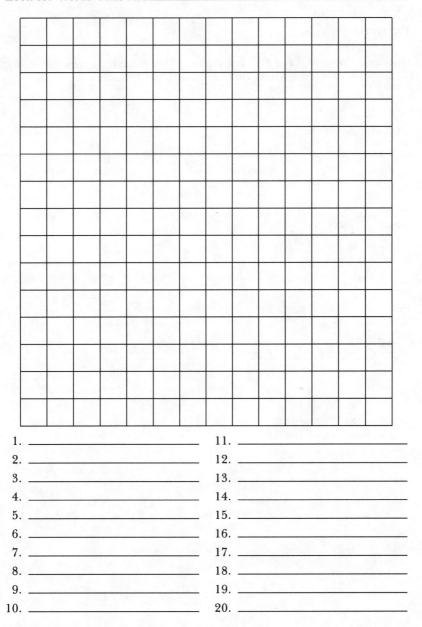

1. ______________________
2. ______________________
3. ______________________
4. ______________________
5. ______________________
6. ______________________
7. ______________________
8. ______________________
9. ______________________
10. ______________________
11. ______________________
12. ______________________
13. ______________________
14. ______________________
15. ______________________
16. ______________________
17. ______________________
18. ______________________
19. ______________________
20. ______________________

Figure 2. Worksheet for creating a word puzzle

may easily be adapted to any grade by changing the type of literature, the centers, and the grouping.

References

Goodman, Yetta M., and Carolyn Burke. 1980. *Reading Strategies: Focus on Comprehension.* New York: Holt, Rinehart, and Winston.

17 Engaging Students with Literature

Robin Auslander Grusko
White Plains High School
White Plains, New York

Students of today are generally passive in their activities and do not understand the teacher's frustrated appeal to them to become involved with their reading of literature. It seems patently absurd to some of them that reading can be an engaging pursuit. It is no easy task to convince them otherwise. I offer three different methods of engaging your students with the text. The common thread running through all of these methods is that even the most blasé students become involved almost in spite of themselves. I have watched the most hardened "I won't do anything" teen become interested.

How do you turn student passivity into activity? One way is to have the characters in the novels come alive. After students have been involved with a novel for a few weeks, they are ready to view the characters. It is important to note that this activity is geared to high school sophomores and juniors who do *not* find it a childish pursuit. Ask for volunteers who will be willing to assume the persona of a character. There are always students ready and willing to do this, or you can appoint some; you will find that students get into their roles very quickly. Any novel lends itself to this activity; for the purpose of this article, I will use *The Scarlet Letter.* Hester, Dimmesdale, Chillingworth, and Pearl are to come alive. Choose two students for each character, because there is often healthy disagreement about why characters act the way they do. In analyzing literature, different interpretations are acceptable as long as they are backed up with reference to the text. These eight students are to think about and write down their character's motivations, desires, and feelings. Other class members write down questions they would like to ask the characters. For example, students want to know why Hester didn't move away, why Dimmesdale allowed Chillingworth to burrow into his heart and soul; they want to know if, in fact, Chillingworth literally poisons Dimmesdale with the herbs that he so assiduously gathers.

Allow time for students to interview the characters. Students who have not taken on personae have not been passive; they have been actively involved in preparing questions, quotations, and statements to which they want characters to respond. The day of the encounter, many of my students dress for their roles. One student, who had taken on the role of Dimmesdale, shocked us all with a minister's coat, collar, and tall black hat. There is interchange between the characters and the class, and also among the eight who have become the characters. Often there are some really tense disagreements. Active engagement: suddenly, students who had decided that Nathaniel Hawthorne is a long-winded bore have to come to terms with the fact that they are enjoying, actually enjoying, his creations.

Another method that engages the entire class in intellectual discovery is the panel discussion. I use this method midway through the year, after the class has read at least four or five novels. Find a common thematic thread that runs through all the books, like courage, or allow the class to discuss and find common themes that could be considered. Divide the class into groups of four. The groups will be involved in an analysis of the nature of the common theme. Here is an example of the assignment, which can easily be modified or expanded.

> This year we have read five novels. A common thematic thread running through each is the courage of the human spirit. In your groups, discuss which character stands out as possessing courage in its purest form and which character exhibits cowardice in its purest form. Your group must be prepared to give a panel discussion to the entire class on [date]. Your report must include your group's definition of courage as well as the reasons why certain characters were rejected for consideration as the most courageous or the most cowardly.
>
> Each person in your group must have a speaking part.
> Person A—definition of courage
> Person B—courageous character
> Person C—cowardly character
> Person D—why other characters were rejected
> (If you have more than four members, arrange to have them contribute with additional ideas.)

I usually devote one week to this activity; each group decides how best to process its time. Students even give themselves homework assignments. Three days for preparation and two or three for delivery are all this activity requires. Once again, interested students are discovering that literature is not just dry stuff. Another advantage to the panel discussion is that as students find relationships between the novels they are also involved in real critical and analytical thought.

The third method of engaging students is one that involves the entire class in lively discussion. I have found this method successful with all levels of students. I discovered it quite accidentally one day when my class had just finished reading a short story. I needed a fresh idea for discussion. We had all been turned to stone by the "answer questions at the end of the story" approach; we were tired of the "short story outline" approach. As we were discussing the significance of the title of the story, I asked the class to look at the title from the point of view of the protagonist and one other character. Would the *characters* think it a good title, or would they prefer another?

We were discussing "The Jilting of Granny Weatherall" by Katherine Anne Porter. The class had a lively debate about whether Granny would have accepted the title readily, or would she have renamed it "The Recovery of Granny Weatherall"? And what about Cornelia? Would Cornelia's title retain the focus on her mother? Some of the topics that we discussed were character development and motivation, the author's tone and purpose, conflict (both internal and external), and theme. The discussion followed an interesting path when one student quoted Shakespeare: "What's in a name? That which we call a rose/By any other name would smell as sweet." Zeroing in on events, details, specifics of the story without the real tedium of "what happened when," my students became aware that literature is alive, vibrant, and accessible.

All of these methods have worked in engaging my students in dialogue with each other, the text, and even themselves. Real critical and creative thinking are important by-products. In *Dimensions of Thinking* (1988), the authors discuss the fostering of thinking skills in our students as the foundation of education:

> Critical and creative thinking . . . are complementary and should be taught in the context of regular academic instruction. Whenever students are formulating a question, analyzing a text, or defining a term with clarity, accuracy, and fair-mindedness, they are developing the skills of critical thinking. Whenever they solve an unstructured problem . . . or plan a project, they are developing their creative abilities. Whenever they consider diverse points of view and imaginatively, empathically, and accurately reconstruct them, they are thinking both creatively and critically. (28)

These three approaches will help your students to connect, critically and creatively, as they become engaged with literature.

Reference

Marzano, Robert J., *et al.* 1988. *Dimensions of Thinking: Framework for Curriculum and Instruction.* Alexandria, Va.: Association for Supervision and Curriculum Development.

18 A Marriage of Form and Content: Teaching *Twelve Angry Men*

Ken Hogarty
Sacred Heart Cathedral Prep
San Francisco, California

Elliot Eisner (1985, 363) maintains, "The history of the curriculum field has been dominated by the aspiration to technologize school and to reduce the need for artistry in teaching." The emergence of reader-response theory and the philosophical grounding on which it stands challenges such domination in the English classroom. The canvas of our classrooms need no longer be sketched with prescribed tracings; rather, the bold strokes of communicatively competent classroom practices can paint richly evocative works of art that echo the aesthetic explorations that are the literary content of our courses from grammar school to college.

In creating such "classroom works of art," teachers might recall some of the principles that guide all artistic endeavor.

Certainly a marriage of form and content, a blending of universal subject and particularized material, and a harmony between artistic intention and the arrested attention of invited participants contribute to the unity of the whole. Such a unity can be creatively wrought in English classes from middle schools to colleges by using or adapting the following one- to two-week unit that focuses on the anthologized television script, *Twelve Angry Men* by Reginald Rose.

I am indebted to Professor William Van Burgess of the University of San Francisco; his use of the play in a graduate education class ("Problem Solving and Decision Making") sketched in the main lines of this unit, an activity I then colored with the hues of a reader-response approach. I find it particularly timely at the beginning of a school year, in that it sets a tone for student communication and interaction, and I have used this activity successfully in eight different classes (honors to remedial) over two years. The play, set entirely in a jury room, is itself about communication and interaction.

Before beginning our reading of the play, I ask students to divide two sheets of paper (front and back) into four equal parts. Twelve of these spaces will be for recording observations and details about each of the characters who are designated by number (e.g., Juror No. 8) rather than by name in the script. The other four spaces are for personal student notes during the reading of the play. These spaces are used as a streamlined version of the usual logs my students keep during reading. One is designated for students to make and update predictions during the course of their reading ("Predictions/ Reorientations"). A second is used to jot down questions that go beyond simple inquiries about factual points ("Questions"). The third is utilized to record feelings, thoughts, and observations that tie in something from the reading with a student's own experience ("Personal Connections"). The last is for other explorations—tie-ins with other works of literature, notations of pertinent or powerful lines, suggestions about the use of symbols—that students might find noteworthy ("Miscellaneous").

After previewing the use of these sheets, I ask students to volunteer for parts to read. While students might not match the actors who played the parts in the original version of *Twelve Angry Men* (Henry Fonda, E. G. Marshall, Jack Klugman, *et al.*), I believe it is important that they read the play aloud rather than view the video version. Along these lines, it provides real dramatic impact to have the student jurors align their desks (or sit around a table) facing each other as if in a jury room. Students not assigned major parts can gather around this "jury table" in close proximity. I have always assigned both boys and girls to roles in the play despite the title.

The play consists of three acts. Each can be read easily during a typical class session, even pausing three or four times during that period to allow students to jot down log entries. I usually start the reading of the play after spending about half the first class period of this unit accomplishing those previewing details noted earlier. Thus, the first act will be concluded with a great deal of time left during the second day of this unit. At the conclusion of the first act, the play's protagonist, who initially had stood alone in voting not guilty in what seems a routinely clear-cut verdict against a young, minority defendant accused of stabbing his own father, has called for a secret ballot to see if any other juror will change his vote to not guilty, thereby continuing the jury's deliberation. By this time, the protagonist has dramatically refuted one assumption important to the case against the defendant, although a great deal of other evidence, including the testimony of two witnesses, would still seem to clearly implicate the boy.

At this point, students are more than ready to discuss what they have been thinking about as the narrative has unfolded and the characters have begun to reveal themselves. I'll usually begin the discussion by inviting students to read their recorded questions and by eliciting student responses. I'll then turn quickly to ask students what they predict will happen in the rest of the play. Invariably, at least one student will predict the actual outcome of the play, that eventually all other eleven jurors will switch their votes and the defendant will be acquitted. After listening noncommittally to various predictions in order to encourage the voicing of this primary exploratory talent of good readers (who mull over many possibilities and are not afraid to seek a constant reorientation during reading), I usually throw out a challenge to the class.

That challenge will usually be phrased something like this: "I'm not going to reveal what the ending is; that's for you to find out as we finish the play. But let's accept, at least hypothetically, the prediction in which all the other jurors switch their votes. After all, as some of you have pointed out, there are still two acts to go, so it doesn't take a crystal ball to predict that someone's going to change his vote. What I want you to do now is to look at your notes and then speculate about the *exact* order in which jurors switch their votes. We know that Juror No. 8 (the protagonist) has voted not guilty in Act One. In what order will the other eleven switch their votes?"

Students are then given papers to individually record their predictions. They are asked not to change these during subsequent activities. Next, students are arbitrarily placed in groups of four to six. These groups are given the rest of the class session and at least another ten minutes at the beginning of the next class period to collaboratively reorient their predictions by deciding on a mutually accepted group response to the same question. The dialogue and negotiation during this activity speak to the inner dialogue that students might replicate in their own readings. Moreover, in echoing the dialogue and negotiation that is the essence of *Twelve Angry Men,* and, by implication, our country's cornerstone of justice, these active "interpretive communities" allow students to see that communicative competence has to do with broadening and expanding horizons intersubjectively rather than just finding facts in isolation. The individual hero of the play is not such because his individuality allows him to stand above society; rather, he is a hero and an individual because he encourages others to individuate themselves for the good of that society.

The second and third acts of the play reiterate such a worldview. As various pieces of evidence are refuted, it is not the protagonist who provides the personal experience from which a questioning of the assumptions of that evidence arises. Rather, different jurors, given confidence to speak up by the rapport established by the hero, do so. That they all speak from a unique experience is an important point not to be lost by students. This reiterates for students that discussions of literature are also enriched by the perspective of many voices, not always the loudest or even the most academically well-informed. Because we all bring different experiences to our explorations of texts, whether they be aesthetic texts or the social texts of our own lives, we can learn more about those texts by encouraging a dialogue with others who have had their own experience with the same or similar texts.

This awareness, along with the interest generated by the speculations about juror vote-switching, leads to a palpable enthusiasm that infuses the class as the rest of the play is read. During that reading, I ask a student to record on the board the order in which jurors actually switch their votes to not guilty. Each switch is accompanied by groans and hurrahs, some individual and some collective. Moving quickly past student "I told you so's" at these junctures, I'll usually use such natural pauses as a time for all students to mark their own logs. Their "Personal Connections" space, heretofore blank in a number of cases, start to get filled as students begin to connect their own deliberations with the deliberations of the jurors about whom they have been reading.

At the end of the play, the class tabulates the individual and collective predictions made two acts earlier. Students are surprised to see that I am more interested in their group scores in relation to their individual scores rather than in a competition between or among various groups or individuals. Students figure the number of places their predictions were "off" the actual order in which jurors switched their votes in the play, so that the best scores, like golf scores, are the lowest (see Figure 1). Thus, with the actual results (first numbers recording the order of voting "not guilty" and the second, preceded by the *J*, the juror number who switched in that sequence) placed against the student and/or group prediction, the final tally is derived by adding the number of places off *each* actual selection is.

Actual Sequence	**Predicted Sequence**	**Score**
1. J8	1. J8	0
2. J9	2. J5	1
3. J5	3. J9	1
4. J2	4. J1	5
5. J6	5. J6	0
6. J11	6. J12	2
7. J7	7. J11	1
8. J12	8. J2	4
9. J1	9. J4	2
10. J10	10. J7	3
11. J4	11. J10	1
12. J3	12. J3	0
		20

Figure 1. Scoring student predictions about juror vote-switching

For a comparison with group scores, students in each group are asked to add all their individual scores (from their own original nonnegotiated predictions) and divide that total by the number of students in the group. In all the classes that I have used this, well over 80 percent of students had a better (lower) group score than individual score, which really gives students pause to think about the benefits of collaboration. Asking the class why this is so always generates quite a response. Students, for example, might point out that only one person in their group figured out that Juror No. 7, who seems so assertive in proclaiming the defendant's guilt in the first act, is not really concerned with the defendant's guilt or innocence; rather, his real motivation is simply to be finished as soon as possible. Thus in retrospect, it is logical that his vote would switch as soon as the majority began voting not guilty. Such an explanation, though easily missed because of taken-for-granted assumptions, is usually quite acceptable to a group if raised by even one member of the group during deliberations. Discussions such as this are, of course, at the heart of students learning to learn about literature from one another.

Even when an individual score is better than that person's group score, interesting discussions usually ensue. Students question the reasons why someone in the group with "better" answers was not heard or drawn out. That student also has to consider whether he or she was assertive enough within the context of the group. Such considerations, in the context of an activity that is usually very relevant for students and one that makes an impression on them, sets the tone for discussions about literature throughout the year.

The concluding activities for this unit can take either one class period or several days. I usually encourage students to write follow-up essays stimulated by their own reading logs or the logs of others. For example, students can pose questions for each other or invite others to respond to connections they have made between the play and other narratives. Characters can be analyzed or compared and contrasted. More germane to the overall intent of this unit, content and form can be married if students are asked to write about the deliberative process, the role of an individual in a group, or leadership considerations, using both the text of the play and the text of students' group experience during this activity. All papers are eventually read aloud, either to the original group or to the class as a whole.

Concluding activities and discussions can take many different turns as students and classes bring their own unique perspectives to the fore and raise this classroom activity to the possibility of artistic endeavor. Since this classroom activity was conceived as a work of art, this shouldn't be surprising. Using the terms of Louise Rosenblatt (1978, ix), a text only becomes a poem (or work of art) when "a reader evokes from it a literary work—sometimes even a literary work of art." A classroom experience as a work of art has to be seen from the same perspective.

One class, for example, reacted strongly to the sexist composition of the jury. The class pursued these questions extensively: How would the play have been different if women were on the jury? Why weren't women on the jury at that time and place? Another class wasn't nearly as inquisitive about the jury's gender: rather, it pursued the analogy between the twelve jurors and the twelve apostles. A very different direction was explored by another class who objected to my "scoring system." Specifically, that class felt that the three jurors who switched their votes virtually interchangeably (Jurors 2, 6, and 11) should have been tallied interchangeably. Such a consideration led to fascinating discussions of statistical data, the so-called objectivity of such data, and the notion of the ways in which facts are generated by "authors." In a fourth class, a very different aesthetic classroom text was painted by students whose transaction with the play's text evoked a consideration of their own personal experiences with the criminal justice system. That class pressed the notion of whether the outcome of the play was realistic or romantic and, by extension, whether the American criminal justice system in today's inner city is a cornerstone of justice for all people in our society.

C. A. Bowers (1984, 2) understands communicative competence as the "outcome of being culturally literate . . . the ability to read or decode the taken-for-granted assumptions and conceptual categories that underlie the individual's world of experience." This play, and the experience it can afford, provides an artistic possibility to evoke such communicative competence. It does so by blending form and content in a way that connects the educational process itself with intersubjective understanding and participation, an ideal that should not be overlooked. Bowers (1984, 31) maintains, "To put it in a manner similar to Dewey's formulation, education, communication, and socialization are nearly interchangeable terms." Men and women concerned with classroom practice need only be angry about classroom activities that divorce these terms and thereby ignore the artistic conception of the texts that are our classrooms.

References

Bowers, C. A. 1984. *The Promise of Theory: Education and the Politics of Cultural Change.* New York: Longman. (Distributed by Teachers College Press.)

Eisner, E. 1985. *The Educational Imagination: On the Design and Evaluation of School Programs.* 2d ed. New York: Macmillan.

Rosenblatt, L. M. 1978. *The Reader, the Text, the Poem: The Transactional Theory of the Literary Work.* Carbondale: Southern Illinois University Press.

19 Using Junior High Readers' Poetry Preferences in the Classroom

Karen Kutiper
Alief Independent School District, Alief, Texas

Richard F. Abrahamson
University of Houston

What poets and poems do junior high school youngsters prefer? In grades 7 through 9, do teenagers say good-bye to poets popular in the elementary school, like Shel Silverstein and Jack Prelutsky, and do these older students opt for Robert Frost, Carl Sandburg, William Stafford, Alfred Lord Tennyson, and other poets who typically find their way into textbook anthologies for this age group?

In order to answer these questions, we turned first to the poetry preference study that has been most quoted in the field for the last fifteen years—Ann Terry's "A National Survey of Children's Poetry Preferences in the Fourth, Fifth, and Sixth Grades" (1977). Researchers have used the Terry study as a model to examine poetry preferences at grade levels from 1 to 12, with the exception of grades 7, 8, and 9. We decided to use the Terry model to fill in the missing piece to the poetry preference puzzle. One major change was made in the Terry design. Terry had students listen to poems that were prerecorded on audiotapes. We felt that the mode of presentation might affect student preferences. Consequently, students in this study were exposed to the selected poems in one of three different ways: one group just listened to the poems read on audiotape; a second group listened to the poems on tape while they read along; the third group just read the poems silently.

In this study, Kutiper (1985) worked with 375 students in grades 7, 8, and 9. The students were exposed to ten poems a day for ten consecutive days. Students rated the poems using a five-point rating scale ranging from "It's great" to "I hate it." They also wrote comments about two of the poems each day.

The 100 poems selected for this study came from several sources. Twenty-five of those poems were the ones selected as most popular in the 1972 Terry study. In the 1979 Bryan-Agee study which used the Terry model, tenth, eleventh, and twelfth graders also chose their favorite poems. Sixty-six of the poems from the Terry study were used in the Bryan-Agee study. Of the favorite 25 poems in the Bryan-Agee study, eight were also favorites in the Terry study. The 17 additional favorites from this top 25 were used in Kutiper's study.

The additional poems for the Kutiper study came from four sources: (1) a middle school/junior high school classroom teacher who enjoys poetry and enjoys teaching poetry; (2) Paul Janeczko, a secondary English teacher who is also an anthologist of contemporary poetry for adolescents; (3) Jack Prelutsky, a contemporary children's poet who is also an anthologist of traditional and contemporary poetry; and (4) Richard Abrahamson, a university professor specializing in the field of adolescent and children's literature. These consultants were asked to recommend poetry that junior high school youngsters might like in the following categories: type of poem (narrative, limerick, lyric, haiku); poetic elements (sounds, imagery, figurative language); content (people, animals, humor, everyday happenings, fantasy, nature, familiar experiences, and social commentary and/or commentary on life); and age of poem (contemporary or traditional).

The purposes of the study were (1) to determine what survey poems were most enjoyed; (2) to analyze the most popular poems considering type, content, and certain poetic elements; (3) to compare relationships between student preferences and their sex and grade level; (4) to compare relationships between student preferences with the preferences of students at other grade levels; and (5) to compare differences in preferences when different modes of presentation were used.

What poems do junior high youngsters enjoy? They certainly have not left behind the poems of childhood. Figure 1 shows the 25 most popular poems in this study. Included in that list are tongue-twisters, limericks, nonsense poems, and two poems each by both Shel Silverstein and Jack Prelutsky. Student responses to the poems in the study, both on the ratings of the individual poems and on the written responses to two poems a day, indicate some very definite likes and dislikes among this age group. The most popular poem type was the narrative. One student wrote on the poetry interest survey prior to the study, "I like poems that tell a story," and this was obviously the feeling of the majority of the subjects. More importantly, they wanted

Title	Author
Sick	Shel Silverstein
Oh, Teddy Bear	Jack Prelutsky
Mother Doesn't Want a Dog	Judith Viorst
Mummy Slept Late and Daddy Fixed Breakfast	John Ciardi
The Unicorn	Shel Silverstein
Why Nobody Pets the Lion at the Zoo	John Ciardi
Homework	Jane Yolen
Dreams	Langston Hughes
Questions	Marcia Ridlon
Willie Ate a Worm Today	Jack Prelutsky
The Ruckus	Dr. Seuss
There Once Was an Old Kangaroo	Edward Mullins
The Young Lady of Niger	Unknown
Peter Piper	Unknown
Eletelephony	Laura Richards
Little Miss Muffet	Paul Dehn
There Was an Old Man of Blackheath	Unknown
Betty Botter	Unknown
Billy Batter	Dennis Lee
Wanting	Unknown
Toot! Toot!	Unknown
Brothers	Bruce Guernsey
Adventures of Isabel	Ogden Nash
We Real Cool	Gwendolyn Brooks
The Cremation of Sam McGee	Robert W. Service

Figure 1. Twenty-five most popular poems in order of preference

that story to be funny, as evidenced by such poems as "Mother Doesn't Want a Dog" and "Mummy Slept Late and Daddy Fixed Breakfast," both found in the top five poems. Only a very few poems in the top 25 could be classified as serious.

The second most popular poetry form was the limerick. Three limericks made their way to the top 25: "There Once Was an Old Kangaroo," "The Young Lady of Niger," and "There Was an Old Man of Blackheath." Comments on student responses support the popularity shown in the ratings. One ninth grader said, "It's so cool and I like limericks because they are so, so dumb." Typical of other responses was this eighth grader's comment: "It's so foolish that it's funny."

Students showed a definite preference for poems that rhymed. The only poem in the top 25 that did not rhyme was Bruce Guernsey's "Brothers," a poignant poem about the tragic death of a young boy as he protected his baby brother. In general, students wanted the poem to be easily understood. This need to understand directly relates to the students' preference for content about familiar, everyday experiences. Students were quick to write comments such as, "I didn't like it because I didn't understand it."

Figurative language often interfered with this need to understand. Students wrote comments about Charles Malem's short poem "Steam Shovel," a familiar poem that compares a steam shovel to a dinosaur whose "jaws were dripping with a load of earth and grass." Written comments indicated the inability of most students at this age not only to appreciate, but also simply to understand, figurative language.

> If the author doesn't realize that it is a machine he's got a problem.
>
> It was dumb. I can't believe he would think a steam shovel is a dinosaur.

The least popular form of poetry was haiku. All six of the haiku in the study rated among the 10 least popular poems. Students' comments about haiku indicate their feelings:

> Whoever wrote this needs to get a new job.
>
> It has no room to say what it means. It's too short to be a poem.

No significant differences between the preferences of boys and girls emerged during the study. Some slight differences for certain poems existed based on content. One favorite of the boys was Jack Prelutsky's "Willie Ate a Worm," in which the heroic Willie swallows "a squiggly, wiggly worm" as "we all stared and we all squirmed." Girls, on the other hand, showed a higher preference for Langston Hughes's poem "Dreams," a poem found in many literature texts and anthologies.

While ninth graders did, overall, prefer poetry less than seventh and eighth graders, their preferences did show some beginnings of change. The older youngsters preferred the limerick less than the other groups. This age group showed a higher preference for poems we could classify as serious. For example "Dreams" was the second most popular poem of this age group. John Updike's poem "Dog's Death," a serious unrhymed poem about the death of a family pet, was the eleventh most popular poem of ninth graders, but did not rate among the 25 most popular poems of seventh and eighth graders.

For the most part, all students at these junior high grades are still exhibiting the preferences of their counterparts in the elementary school.

Modes of Presentation

One part of the investigation unique to this study was an examination of the modes of poetry presentation. The students at each grade level were divided into three distinct groups. One group listened to the poems on audiotape. Another group listened to the poems and read them simultaneously, and a third group only read the poems. Because of the educational traditions of "You follow along in your textbook while you listen to Robert Frost read this poem," or "You follow along in your textbook while you listen to me (or a classmate) read this poem, then we'll discuss it," we expected to find the highest preferences for poetry in the group that listened to the poems at the same time they read them. In the top 25 poems, there were no differences in degree of preference according to mode of presentation. Favorites were favorites no matter how they were presented. However, this was not the case elsewhere.

In 53 of the remaining 75 cases, there was a significant difference in preference according to the mode of presentation. In 51 of those cases, students who only read the poems without hearing them gave higher ratings to the poems. In 37 cases, students who listened to the poems and read them simultaneously gave the poems the lowest ratings. In other words, students seemed to indicate they would rather read the poems by themselves without the interference of any other modality. These results indicate that as classroom teachers we should examine how we present poetry to students. Not all poems are meant to be heard.

Interestingly enough, all of the 25 least popular poems were serious poems, poems without rhyme or rhythm, or poems with unusual forms. Students who only read those poems gave higher ratings to 13 of the 18 poems, showing a significant statistical difference in degree of preference. Time to read a poem silently seems to be a most important instructional consideration when working with serious unrhymed poetry.

In summary, this study adds to the existing knowledge in the field of poetry preferences in two ways. It updated and confirmed adolescent poetry preferences. Second, it explored for the first time the relationship of mode of poetry presentation to the degree of preference.

If we are ever to raise students' interest in the genre of poetry, we cannot ignore their own preferences. We must start with those preferences, building a firm foundation, before moving students toward more sophisticated poetry. Classroom teachers must be aware of student preferences, letting them guide the selection of poems for sharing in the classroom. We must then attempt carefully to turn those preferences into real interest in the genre. The fact that the serious, the contemplative, or the different poem might never be popular with students should not limit exposure to only those poems that are currently popular with students. While preferences of seventh, eighth, and ninth graders can be used as a beginning, a balance must be maintained to keep students interested in poetry while developing a keener sense of appreciation. Teachers should work to expand poetry interests by careful selection of poems for classroom use. One instructional suggestion might be to pair a popular poem with a more traditional or stylistically original poem that has similar content. Sharing the popular or "fun" poetry and teaching the more difficult or abstract will only increase the dichotomy now existing. Students should have pleasurable sharing experiences with more difficult, more sophisticated, and less predictable poetry before undertaking poetry explication, a task that all too often brings a student his or her only contact with poetry.

Prior to taking part in this study, students completed a survey that revealed their interests in poetry but also provided an outlet for some of their feelings about the genre and how it is handled. In closing, here are some revealing comments to the following completion stem: *A teacher who wants children to like poetry should*

- Let them choose their own poetry
- Give them poetry about subjects they like
- Teach them some funny poems
- Read them more poems
- Give them a chance to read poems they like first and then teach them new kinds of poetry

References

Bryan, M. A., and H. Agee. 1979. Poetry Preferences among High School Students. Dissertation, University of Georgia.

Kutiper, K. S. 1985. A Survey of the Adolescent Poetry Preferences of Seventh, Eighth, and Ninth Graders. Doctoral dissertation, University of Houston.

Terry, C. A. 1972. A National Survey of Children's Poetry Preferences in the Fourth, Fifth, and Sixth Grades. Doctoral dissertation, The Ohio State University.

20 Deconstructing the Multiple-Choice Test

Thomas McKendy
Marianopolis College

A couple of years ago when I was teaching *Wuthering Heights,* my friend Rick Adams pulled from his files an old test that a friend of his had come across as a student teacher. Some of the questions required simple identifications: "What is Catherine's 'narrow home out yonder'?" or "Who is referred to as 'the little canary'?" Others were a little tougher:

The character Heathcliff can *best* be described as
a. a unique but quite believable personality.
b. an evil emissary from Satan.
c. a cuckoo.
d. a living principle of the elemental in man.

Lockwood's role in the novel is essentially that of
a. a scapegoat.
b. a mere technical device.
c. an outsider whose personality provides a contrast with the major characters.
d. an essential secondary character.

Questions like these drive me crazy. Lockwood, for example, is no scapegoat and as a technical device he is anything but mere. Worse yet, the last two choices suggest that Lockwood is not even a major character. I began to rant. Since none of the choices is right—and none perhaps wholly wrong—the teacher was unfairly expecting high school students to make complex and arbitrary discriminations.

Rick is always calmer than I am. The test was not unfair, he said, but was probably very easy. The students were being asked simply to provide the answer that had been given *in the notes.* Of course. In fact, even though I had not been in the class, even though I did not have the notes, I was now pretty sure of the right answer to each question. Which answer sounds like something a teacher would say? Which answer would be least likely to spring spontaneously from classroom discussion? Which answer is the longest?

I began to rant again. Poor preparation for college! Mockery of education! Idea that there's one right answer!

Rick stopped me again. Maybe this guy's a genius, he said. You know how kids act like lawyers. They'll argue all day to get one more point on a test. So he makes up a test full of plausible answers, arbitrarily marks one right, and then hands back the test. Presto. A lively class discussion. If you walk into a class and say "What is Emily Bronte's primary concern in *Wuthering Heights,*" what do you get? Silence. Yawns. Instead, give a test with a question like this:

> The novel illustrates that Emily Bronte was primarily concerned with
> a. man and society.
> b. man and God.
> c. man's unity with nature.
> d. man's prejudices.

Mark *d* right and watch what happens when you hand back the test. The students will even back up their ideas with evidence from the text if they think they can raise their grades. If you're really feeling wicked, announce that the discussion has persuaded you and that those who originally chose *d* will now lose a point.

Give it a try, I thought. So I brought Rick's old test into my class and put it on the overhead near the end of the hour:

> Which set of polarities best describes the major love relationships in the novel?
> a. good vs. evil.
> b. mutable vs. immutable.
> c. life vs. death.
> d. spontaneous vs. gradual.
>
> The inclusion of such devices as diaries and letters is significant because they
> a. relieve the monotony of Nelly's narration.
> b. are convenient means to speed up the story.
> c. relate exciting episodes.
> d. provide fresh perspectives and authenticity.

As the editors of the Sunday papers know, almost everyone likes a quiz, and my students actually debated about the narrative techniques and major love relationships in *Wuthering Heights.*

Now none of this was enough to make me start giving multiple-choice tests. After all, if kids do not write in English class, where will they write? But I did start bringing in multiple-choice questions at the beginning of class to warm up a discussion. Sometimes I even had students write brief explanations for their choices. Once I got so carried away that I tried a multiple-choice essay topic in my Shakespeare course:

> Write an essay on Shakespeare's portrayal of love, marriage, romance, the war between the sexes. You should deal mainly with *Love's Labour's Lost, The Taming of the Shrew,* and *Romeo and Juliet,* and you may want to deal with such issues as those suggested by the following multiple-choice questions:
>
> In Shakespeare's early plays love is
>
> a. a superficial relationship based on looks.
> b. a superficial relationship based on money.
> c. absolute selflessness.
> d. a source of self-knowledge.
> e. a kind of naive blindness based on self-deception and ignorance of others.
> f. a courtly ritual detached from feelings.
> g. a romantic fiction that disintegrates in the face of social realities.
> h. an innocent and beautiful awakening to the possibilities of life.
> i. a Petrarchan pose.
> j. a powerful force that creates harmony.
> k. a social convenience that makes possible the political and economic relations implicit in the society.
> l. a one-way relationship without much communication.
> m. a chance to show off verbal skills.

I no longer remember when I first realized that my students knew more about multiple-choice questions than I did. What the sonnet was to Shakespeare's contemporaries the multiple-choice question is to students of our time. They've read a million of them. They understand the conventions of the genre: the rules, the variations, the nuances, and the tricks.

I began to ask them to write the questions, perhaps five or six apiece at the end of each book or unit:

> According to Mr. Bounderby [in *Hard Times*], every hand's ambition is to
>
> a. live like a king and act like a dog.
> b. be happy and fulfilled.
> c. take over Coketown and all its money and factories.

d. work long hard hours and accept what pay is given to them.
e. feed on turtle soup and venison with a gold spoon.

Which is the correct sequence of the deaths of these characters:
a. Polonius, Claudius, Gertrude, Hamlet's father, Ophelia, Hamlet, Laertes?
b. Hamlet's father, Ophelia, Polonius, Laertes, Claudius, Gertrude, Hamlet?
c. Hamlet's father, Polonius, Ophelia, Gertrude, Claudius, Laertes, Hamlet?
d. Claudius, Laertes, Polonius, Ophelia, Hamlet's father, Gertrude, Hamlet?
e. Polonius, Hamlet's father, Gertrude, Claudius, Laertes, Hamlet, Ophelia?
f. Hamlet's father, Polonius, Gertrude, Ophelia, Laertes, Claudius, Hamlet?

To write such questions sometimes involves only careful review—thankfully my student omitted Guildenstern and gentle Rosencrantz—but often understanding and interpretation are at issue as well:

Which person would Thoreau most admire?
a. a vagabond who is also an alcoholic.
b. a gypsy who owns a horse and a tent.
c. a wealthy man with a house in every city in the world.
d. a hard-working young lawyer.
e. a student not getting enough sleep because he has to write English assignments every night.

A poet's primary objective in a poem is
a. to explain a fact.
b. to convey a meaning.
c. to evoke emotion.
d. to give the reader something to puzzle over.

Questions like these will provoke more classroom debate than any question the teacher could have asked. Now the student writer is the judge and you, as teacher, are merely one of the lawyers presenting arguments. If at times you find none of the answers acceptable, don't rant. Remember my friend Rick. Defend your position with evidence from the text, and choose the phrase that *best* completes the following sentence:

Student-written multiple-choice questions may be used as

a. a way of stimulating class discussion.
b. a means of review for question writers and their classmates.
c. an opportunity for teachers to identify areas that need further discussion or clarification.
d. a writing prompt for essays or other assignments.
e. a writing exercise that students enjoy.

21 Cowboys, Cowgirls, and Literary Criticism

Anne Sherrill
East Tennessee State University

As we attempt to get high school or college students to appreciate well-written literature, the usual approach is to call attention to effective passages of description, dialogue, and other literary elements that contribute to the success of the work. We hope that by seeing good examples, students will be able to discriminate between the good and not so good. But why not work from the opposite direction? Offer them a poorly written story such as the one that follows. They can have some fun discussing it and setting up some basic criteria for judging quality in fiction.

The Brave Ones
by M. C. Burillark†

A mist hung over the sleepy Western town. As it cleared away, the tall fronts of the bank, the saloon, the sheriff's office clearly jutted above the vast expanse of lone prairie. Down the main street Rock Gibralter and Melanie O'Murphy were strolling hand in hand.

Rocky was Pine Gulch's sheriff—a handsome man with bronzed face and arms, sunbleached hair, and a commanding stature. His clear, dark blue eyes were gazing at Melanie—a beautiful girl with curly, golden hair, light blue eyes, and fair pink skin.

In her soft, sweet voice Melanie exclaimed, "Oh, Rocky, I do wish the stage would arrive. And I wish that it would bring my uncle rather than his money. Poor thing. But it was dear of him to leave me such a nice inheritance." Rock shifted his gaze from her face to the main road and spotted the stage arriving amidst thundering hooves and a cloud of dust.

A child was playing in the street ruts sweetly oblivious to his approaching destruction. Without a thought for his own safety,

† M. C. Burillark is a pseudonym for Anne Sherrill, Helen Burt, and Ellen Temple, who wrote an earlier version of "The Brave Ones" for use in English classes at Bellaire High School in Houston, Texas.

Rock sprang for the child, flung him from the stage's path, and rolled away in the nick of time as the crushing wheels roared by. As the child scampered off, the townspeople rushed to commend Rock for his heroic feat. Melanie glowed with pride.

After he and Melanie had safely deposited her money in the bank, Rock was called upon to preserve law and order at the saloon where a fight had broken out. In the meantime there was more than the usual activity outside the bank. Five men dressed in black burst through the door, guns blazing, arms bulging with loot. How sinister they looked with their greasy hair, black hats, and rumpled shirts. The commotion aroused the sleeping deputy sheriff who, within seconds, shot at one of the robbers making his escape. A black horse stumbled and a wounded villain fell to the ground. Rock emerged from the saloon in time to see the men riding off looking like an enormous black cloud of dust on the horizon. At Rock's whistle, Bullet galloped to his side. With a leap, Rock was on the gallant Bullet's back and the two disappeared—blond hair, white tail and mane streaming in the wind.

Meanwhile, back in the dusty street, Johnny James writhed in agony. The bullet from the deputy's gun had grazed his right knee, ricocheted off and then lodged in his left calf. Still it took the strength of three deputies to get Johnny James into the jailhouse. As he kicked and screamed, it seemed that the scar on his left cheek turned a deep purple.

The deputy wasted no time in questioning him. "Who's your leader? Where are they taking the money?"

Johnny scowled, "I refuse to answer on the grounds that it might tend to incriminate me."

The next morning the sun seemed to shine with a peculiar, strong, illuminating light. Johnny James had risen early. The throb in his leg continued. He lighted a cigarette and hobbled over to the window. His eye quickly surveyed the scene outside. There was only one person up at this early hour and strangely enough, it was a little child playing with his imaginary horse in the street. Johnny looked only briefly at the child, yet somehow, for some reason, his eyes kept returning. He was humming a tune—a familiar tune. If he would only come closer so Johnny could hear.

Suddenly the child stopped and stooped down. He had picked up something. Then suddenly, as if from heaven, a shaft of light fell on the little scene. The child's face was the picture of innocence and youth and helpfulness. Something stirred in Johnny's breast. A forgotten longing, a remembrance, such strange feelings for a ruthless criminal.

Then Johnny saw what this child of innocence and sweetness had in his hand. A baby sparrow, a little sparrow that had been learning to fly but had fallen. Gently, the child placed the baby sparrow back in its nest.

For a moment, time seemed to stand still. The shaft of light, the innocent child, the baby sparrow, and the strange hidden longings within a criminal. And just as suddenly, it was over. The child ran on his merry way down the street, and Johnny turned back to his cell. But it was not the old Johnny. Perhaps this was the real Johnny.

Johnny James knew immediately what he must do. "Sheriff," he called. "Sheriff, come quickly. I have a confession to make."

Moments later, still in the early morning hours, the posse was on its way to help Rock Gibralter.

Much had happened to Rock since he and Bullet sped like lightning in quest of the men who had taken the money of the good people of Pine Gulch. As the sun grew hotter, Rock grew thirsty. He had forgotten his canteen! He and Bullet had had to interrupt their journey earlier, for Bullet stuck a thorn in his hoof. After carefully removing it, Rock rode again. But precious time had been lost. Toward evening, Rock and Bullet rested under an oak tree. Even Bullet felt the sting of thirst, for he gave forth with his familiar whinny, the one he gave when he needed water or food or rest.

As the sun began to drop on the horizon, the air grew cooler. Rock built a fire to warm Bullet and then set out in search of food. After walking a few yards from the fire, Rock suddenly spied a prairie buffalo. One shot from his six-gun and the buffalo lay on the ground. He dragged the animal toward the fire. As he did so, his eye spied an old sword that was perfect to use as a spit. But Rock was the kind of man who pondered over unexplainable things. What was the sword doing there? It must be a mark of some sort. He would investigate after dinner.

The aroma of the roasting buffalo brought the smart to Rock's mouth—no water. Bullet, as if reading his thoughts, broke the stillness of the night with his familiar whinny.

When the buffalo was done, Rock offered Bullet his share and then sat down to eat. The food choked him. There was no water.

Suddenly Rock's ears heard a rustling several yards away in the same direction the sword had been pointing. Stealthily he crept toward the sound, keeping exactly in line with the direction the sword had pointed. To Rock, it seemed as if he crept a mile. His throat ached, but soon he saw an outline against the black night. A cabin!

As he drew closer, he saw a light inside and peeped into a window. Seated around a round, wooden table were four men. Rock recognized the jagged scar over the right eye of one of the robbers—and the black gloves and the swarthy grin. He strained to hear the conversation.

"No, fellers, that light weren't nothin' but some feller eatin' his buffalo meat. Boy howdy! What I kin do with this loot!"

"Ah, shut up. We ain't even counted it yit."

"All right, men, I'll take charge. Lefty, hand me the bills first."

"This here is marked for a Miss Melanie O'Murphy, Blackie."

"I was right," thought Rock. "They are the robbers!"

Suddenly, one man rose slowly, then like a flash of lightning drew his six-gun.

"OK, stand back. I'm taking the loot."

Lunging at him, another man cried, "You double-crosser!"

The gun went off. The bullet hit an old pine door, then ricocheted into the double-crosser's breast. He fell to the floor, dead.

"Hey, boys, did you hear that noise at the winder?"

Before Rock could hide, two men had discovered him. One man hit him from behind. Rock was unconscious!

He woke up bound and gagged, gazing into the eyes of three unshaven men.

"Well, if it ain't the sherriff of Pine Gulch all tied up. Take the gag outta his mouth. Watcha got to say fer yerself now?"

"Nothing," replied Rock staunchly.

However, Rock was not wasting time. He had wrenched one hand free—but his left hand. It was weak from an old wound.

"Say, men, could I please have some water?" Rock inquired politely.

"Why, shore, that cain't hurt nothin', think Blackie?"

"No, go ahead."

As the robber held the tin cup to Rock's lips, he hurled his left fist straight into the bandit's jaw. Stunned, the outlaw fell to the floor, unconscious. A second man lunged at Rock but he kicked him securely in the head. Another fell to the floor. The third man leaped for his gun but fell over the dead robber. Quicker than lightning, Rock rolled over to where the man was stumbling to his feet. Rock's first swing missed. His attempted kick, feet still bound securely, missed. The robber grabbed his gun and fired. Stunned, Rock fell to the floor, wounded in the left shoulder. The man hovered over him, gun in hand. Rock remembered an old trick he had learned from his pa. This would be his last try, for he was weakening. Gathering all his strength he knocked the villain unconscious with a karate chop given with the heel of his boot.

He rolled over to where the gun lay then propped himself against the wall, his strength ebbing. What if the posse found his trail? They would not find the cabin, for the sword was gone. Suddenly Rock heard Bullet's familiar whinny. But then came an anxious whinny. Rock knew it well from other times when they had shared trouble. Bullet was worried. Rock sent him a telepathic message.

"Bullet, old boy. Go back to the fire. The fire, old boy. The posse will find you."

Rock leaned heavily against the wall now, but through a blur he thought he saw Bullet gallop into the darkness of night. Time passed. The sun rose in the morning sky as Rock grew weaker. At times he felt so weak he could barely hold the gun, but his steady eyes never betrayed his condition to the now conscious robbers. Rock thought of Bullet. Where was his old friend? Suddenly, sometime that afternoon thundering up to the cabin came the posse led by Bullet.

"Rock, you OK?" inquired one of the men as he burst through the cabin door.

"Yes," nodded Rock. Suddenly all his strength returned.

"Here they are," he said, motioning to the robbers. "Let's get back to town. Thanks for coming, boys."

The entire town of Pine Gulch honored Rock Gibralter two days later. Bands played and a parade was staged. At his side as he stood to thank the townfolk was Melanie O'Murphy.

"I'm so proud of my own little hero, Rock. To think what could have happened to you with those mean ole robbers."

"Aw, shucks, Melanie," Rock said gazing at her fondly, "my life wouldn't matter much if I didn't have you."

The End

The basic elements of any short story are present in "The Brave Ones," but examples abound for a study of flaws in quality.

The plot is fraught with coincidence. Rock happens to find an old sword that serves as a spit for the buffalo and also points in the direction of the cabin. A frequent ploy in formula fiction, there also is plot manipulation, the creation of incidents not part of the main storyline but present to show off the character of the hero. The rescue of the child playing in the path of the stagecoach is a good example. The story follows the classic plot outline with complicating incident, rising action, climax (perhaps several), and falling action, but students should easily see that the story is hackneyed in the old-fashioned Western sense.

All the characters including Bullet are stock. They resemble warehouse characters who can be readily taken off a shelf and summed up in a single sentence. Students will recognize the strong handsome sheriff, the pretty blond girlfriend, the sleeping deputy, and ugly villains with scars and black hats.

The story also presents an opportunity to discuss character change. Logic dictates that changes be believable and reflect sufficient time and motivation. A hardened criminal like Johnny James would probably not be moved to confession by seeing a child helping a sparrow.

The language attached to some of the characters is stilted, another signal of poorly crafted fiction. Johnny James speaks this way, as does one of the other robbers whose language contrasts ineffectively with the author's attempt at dialect in the others.

Students can make a list of trite descriptions such as "quick as lightning," "thundering hooves," and "cloud of dust." Other ingredients that should get a chuckle include the child's being able to handily reach the sparrow's nest, ricocheting bullets, and a horse that eats meat and receives telepathic messages.

Students might enjoy discussing TV westerns or movies that depart from the stereotypes exemplified in "The Brave Ones."

Laughing at an outrageously poor story offers students some security in their own taste. It makes an introduction to literary criticism more than an academic exercise. And hopefully they will begin to approach their reading with another slant to the question, "Was it any good?"

22 Listening: An Invitation to Literacy

Wendy Rodgers Clark
Shelter Island USFD
Shelter Island, New York

My first graders sprawl in assorted postures around my feet, wide-eyed, leaning into the words. I am reading from Meindert DeJong's *The Wheel on the School* (1954, Harper and Row):

> The women of Shora rushed up the dike steps, dreading what they might see on the other side.
>
> On top of the dike the women stood in a row and stared into the distance where the old, upturned boat loomed. On the boat they could see the stooped figure of [old] Douwa. He was kneeling and sawing with all his might.
>
> "But where's Lina?" Lina's mother demanded.
>
> The women searched the empty strand, but there was no girl anywhere in sight in all the dry distance of the sea bottom. "Oh, no!" a woman exclaimed suddenly. She pointed. "Isn't that the tide coming in?"

Agitated murmurs ripple through my audience. We have already talked about the fierce tides in the Netherlands. Eileen sits up straighter, hugging herself. "Hurry!" she whispers. I continue:

> Far away toward the islands and almost beyond their sight, a thin crawling silvery line was forming. "There!" the pointing woman said urgently. "Can't you see it? Over there, right over against the islands."
>
> "It is the tide!" Another woman saw it at last. "The tide's coming. We've got to get Douwa down from that boat before he gets cut off from the dike. At high tide that whole boat goes under."
>
> They ran. They ran clumsily in their billowing, heavy skirts and wooden shoes. The tide was faster. The thin, innocent-looking silvery line, that had been so far away it could hardly be seen, came with a slithering, snaky rush. Right behind the ground tide rushed the deeper tide, deepening moment by

> moment until, far out at sea, a great wall of water formed itself and came roaring toward the land. (151)

As I close the book with exaggerated reluctance, I am blasted with a chorus of protests:

"Aaaaw, Mrs. Clark!"

"Come on, don't stop yet!"

"Just one more page! Please?"

These children are insistent because they know what the women on the dike do not: The small girl, Lina, is at this very moment trapped beneath the upturned boat and has only seconds to make her escape.

So I relent and read to the end of the same page:

> . . . the first hissing line of bottom water slid swiftly under the boat and curled coldly around her toes. Lina gasped. "Oh, it's here," she yelled. "The water's here."

I pause and glance up.

There are groans. "Oh, no! I bet you're *really* going to stop there!"

Carefully, I insert the bookmark, smiling. "How did you ever know?"

"Because you *always* do that!"

And they are right. I always do *that*—just as my own third-grade teacher did (bless her!) when she read *The Wheel on the School* aloud to my class in 1955, the year it won the Newbery Award. A child once said that something becomes your own when "it goes down in your heart and gets stuck there." This book got stuck in my heart way back then, and each year I use it in my classroom, knowing that other children will make it their own.

Rationale

I believe that listening is the key to literacy. Children learn to speak because they are surrounded by talk. But effective writing is more than just talk written down; good stories are quite different from ordinary conversation in that they have a formal structure and require listeners/readers to exercise their imaginations. All children thirst for knowledge and are constantly refining and redefining what they know in terms of new information. Listening and talking provide opportunities for them to make meanings. But stories offer them something more, because the written word has the capacity to feed children's appetite for images—images to be stored up and called upon as they learn to write and read.

By reading aloud, we help children to construct bridges to literacy by inviting them to use their imaginations and to make personal connections. While it is important to share stories that reflect and confirm the familiar, it is also important to provide narrative experiences that expand and challenge existing perceptions.

I am convinced that chapter books should be included in the materials we select to share with young children. Chapter books call for deeper levels of understanding and commitment because they allow children to become involved with plot and characters over a period of time and encourage them to reach beyond pictures and print for meaning. Children recall, predict, infer, anticipate, empathize, agonize, and celebrate—and they do all this without thinking about it! Long before children can tackle such books on their own, we need to be tuning the mind's ear and opening the mind's eye to really good literature—and we need to continue, long after children are capable of reading to themselves.

Reading

My first graders know that snack time is chapter book time. When I pass out the crackers, they get settled in a comfortable position "so you can listen with your whole self." Some children devour their snack, others nibble the edges to make it last. I tell them good books are like that: We gobble picture books right up, but chapter books are meant to be tasted a little at a time.

On the day I begin reading *The Wheel on the School,* I bring in a large pair of wooden shoes and encourage the children to handle them and try them on, saying we will all be walking somewhere in them very soon. Later, when we are gathered on the rug, I explain that this story takes place in a time before cars or telephones were invented, in a town so small that the whole school has only one girl and five boys. It happens halfway around the world in a country so low and flat that, even today, dikes must hold back the sea and canals lace the land. Soon we are launched on the great adventure.

It all begins with Lina. She writes a composition about storks that sets her teacher and classmates wondering: Why don't the huge birds with their happy, clacking bills come to nest in Shora as they do in other villages nearby? Her teacher has the great wisdom to close school an hour early on the promise the children will wonder about Lina's question because "sometimes when we wonder we can make things begin to happen." Sure enough, things begin to happen.

DeJong's use of imagery and his skillful characterization endear this book to me. As I read, I will often say to the children, "You might want to close your eyes for this part so you can make a picture in your head. Can you see Dirk's hand creeping over the wall? Can you smell the sea? Taste the salt? Hear the wind wailing?" Young children have absolutely no reservations about this sort of thing. "I can see it!" They sniff huge gulps, lick their lips. The imagery becomes palpable.

The structure of *The Wheel on the School* invites ongoing enthusiasm and involvement. Lina and the boys must find a wagon wheel for use as a nesting platform in order to lure storks back to Shora. The children set off to search in places "where a wheel could be and where one couldn't possibly be." The latter is, of course, where one is finally found. Their separate paths lead to extraordinary mishap, mirth, and mischief, and gradually circle back, converging, careening toward the heart-stopping climax.

Reach

From the start, children are connecting and extending, and I follow their lead as they reach for understanding. They confirm ("I know what that is!"), they compare ("That's sort of like . . ."), they question ("How big *is* a stork?"). I respond ("Isn't she brave?"), I support ("Good idea! You're probably right!"), I provoke ("Do you think it's fair that girls aren't allowed to vault canals with the boys?").

As the story unfolds, I find myself exploring and inquiring along with my young audience: How do such big birds fly? Where is Shora? How can a dike hold back the sea? Why do windmills turn? How would it feel to have no legs? Do you know anyone as old as Douwa? Are there any storks in the United States? What does a trundle bed look like? Will sucking a wineball make you drunk? How come they wear wooden shoes?

The language, the setting, the events linger in the classroom long after I have closed the book. It's as if the story has settled into the very souls of the children: Dave tells Brian, who can't find his eraser, to "look where it could be and where it couldn't possibly be." After I read how Lina stares into her wooden shoe to help her think better, there is Bree, peering into her sneaker at math time. "Hey! It really works, Mrs. Clark!" Children color flags of Holland to decorate their desks. They search the map of Europe for the place I have marked. In the block corner there are dikes and clock towers; rug scraps have become the sea.

Journals hold drawings and references to the novel, and the puppets come alive, muttering "impossibly impossible!" Always, there are children stealing moments at the chalkledge where the book is propped enticingly between readings. They peek at the soft black-and-white illustrations by Maurice Sendak, find words they can read. They guess excitedly about what might happen next and come to whisper in my ear. I play innocent. "Do you think so? Could it be?"

Response

Over the years, the response to *The Wheel on the School* has been rich and varied. But one year it took on magical proportions. That year we finished the last chapter just two weeks before our school's annual Book Character Day, and my children and classroom became the children and setting from this special book.

"Let's all dress up like the guys from *The Wheel on the School*!" Christopher suggested.

"But there aren't enough parts to go around!" Kimberley wanted to be Lina.

The children counted while I listed characters on the board. There were enough, though it would mean some children taking lesser roles. "Not everyone can be Lina or Janus," I reminded them.

"We could draw straws!"

I applauded their idea and suggested that older children who had heard the book when they were in my class might especially enjoy seeing the familiar characters. "What could we do to make it come alive?" I asked.

"We could make pictures!"

"Put on a puppet show!"

"Build a dike—and a *humongous* clock tower!"

I chuckled at their enthusiasm. "It almost sounds as if you want to turn our classroom into the town of Shora."

There was a split second of silence, then a unanimous roar, "Hey, yeah! We *could* do that!"

In the animated discussion that followed, they decided to dramatize parts of the novel using the entire room as a stage. Those who did not get to play a lead role would have their choice of sets to build.

"We can't do the whole story," I said. "What are your favorite parts?"

"When Elka gets pulled halfway out the hayloft and the rope breaks!"

"When Big Jella almost drowns in the canal!"

"When Old Douwa's father is shipwrecked and has to eat slimy crabs and things!"

"When the tots climb the rickety ladder and get trapped in the tower under the bell!"

"When the twins are pushing the wheelchair, and Legless Janus is hollering, 'Out of the way, all you mortals!' "

"When they have to rescue the drowning storks before the tide comes!"

These children need no prompting; the ideas tumble out. I write hurriedly on the board. Later we will talk about which ones are feasible, and the children will work in teams to make it happen. Parents, too, will be caught up in the preparation.

Result

On Book Character Day, all classes receive a written invitation to "travel around the world and step back in time." Visitors enter through the Dutch doorway, cut in a large cardboard windmill that covers the entrance to our classroom.

The dike, a line of desks piled down the middle of the room and draped with green fabric, dominates the scene. Swirls of blue chalk transform the chalkboard into the sea. There is salty glasswort to taste. The erstwhile bookloft now sports wisps of hay and a thick rope with its frayed end dangling. An erector-set clock tower rises in one corner. Canals are shaped with tumbled chairs.

Erik kneels on the seat of my teacher's chair, his legs bent in half and thrust into his father's pants which are pinned under him. He grips large paper wheels attached to each side. Kerry and Michael have managed to locate wooden shoes, and Jason wears a cloth cap just like the ones illustrated. All the girls wear paper hats they have "embroidered" with crayon designs.

A low bookshelf, stuffed with pillow and comforter, has become a trundle bed. Parents have supplied authentic props—there are bright tulips in a Delft vase and the aroma of fresh bread tickles our nostrils. Paper storks, wings wired wide, hang suspended from the lights. And there, balanced on the tall bookshelf, is a real wagon wheel.

We ask our audience, seated along one wall, to "squint your eyes and use your imagination," but there is no need. Each tableau is spellbinding. The children ad-lib, sometimes interjecting an explanatory aside. My brief narration smoothes the transition between scenes. The audience is absorbed and appreciative. And for this day, we have all become as one with the characters in *The Wheel on the School.*

Although this novel is recommended reading for Grade 5 and up, I believe it is a timeless story for all ages. DeJong has bridged generations, cultures, and continents to reveal basic truths about the universality of human nature and the connectedness of the human race.

If we are to help children make connections to good literature, we first must be knowledgeable advocates of what is really good. The *Wheel on the School* is just one of many such books that endure, bringing joy and insight to the listener/reader. It has worked its magic for me during ten years of teaching. Each time I read it, the magic works. Good books never lose their flavor; to the contrary, they seem to get better with age.

23 Action Books as Story Retelling Prompts

Gerry Bohning
Barry University

Story retelling is a recommended instructional technique in the primary classroom because it actively involves children with literature. Retelling requires children to listen to a story, prepare a retelling, and then present their own personal interpretation. The retelling becomes a rewarding social opportunity as children communicate with their audiences. Children who share stories through retelling become excited about language and books.

Story retelling can significantly improve children's story comprehension, sense of story structure, and oral language competency—skills that are critical for success in school (Garnett 1986; Morrow 1985). Story retelling builds the foundation for more sophisticated expressive language tasks: discussing, explaining, and reporting. Retelling also gives the teacher diagnostic information. The way students structure retellings gives information about when comprehension and oral language development are proceeding smoothly and when they are not (Goodman 1982).

If the benefits of story retelling are to accrue, there must be guided practice opportunities for children. One way to get started with story retelling in the primary classroom (K–3) is to use action books as prompts.

Action Books

Action books are often called pop-ups or movable books. They have three-dimensional scenes, pop-ups, cut-outs, lift-flaps, or other movements to accompany the story. The books have tremendous eye appeal, and it is this attractive format that makes them so inviting for beginning story retellings. They invite student attention and repeated use. Peter Seymour's *The Animals' Surprise* has animals parade through a cut-out frame on each page as they bring food to a wonderful party. Children never tire of telling or listening to this story because the wonderful party is for them.

Beginning story retellers tend to omit the setting, enumerate without elaboration, leave out important events, sequence incorrectly, or end a story inappropriately (Garnett 1986; Morrow 1985). Children need help understanding and expressing the organization of the stories they hear. The three-dimensionals in action books are especially well-suited as prompts for beginning story retellers. The visuals serve as mental reminders. They hold the attention of the audience and help children sequence the story and become more self-confident in the initial retelling situations.

The Strategy: Retelling with Prompts

Story retelling with three-dimensional prompts is a six-step teaching strategy based on techniques suggested from the research reported by Garnett (1986), Goodman (1982), Koskinen (1988), and Morrow (1985). Frequent small-group retelling opportunities are necessary so children have chances to practice and improve their skills over time. At first, story retellings will be brief but will become longer as children gradually develop the expressive language and story organizational skills to carry out the activity.

Story Selection

Select books for initial story retellings that are short and have plenty of action. They should be interesting to listen to and fun to retell. The "All-Action Treasure Hour" series is a set of six favorite fairy tales, each with three-dimensional scenes that fold out as the pages are turned. This simple and sturdy design is ideal for beginning retellings. Or, you may prefer to begin the retelling activities with wordless action books and invent the story as you go along. John Goodall's *Paddy Finds a Job* offers humorous situations for retelling. The resource bibliography at the end of this chapter lists action books to get you started.

With the children, set a purpose for listening. Explain that you will be reading a story and later they will be asked to retell it in their own words. Explain that story retelling will help them understand the story better and improve their language skills.

Story Discussion

After reading the book to a small group, talk with the children about the story. This discussion is needed for reflecting, reacting, probing characters' feelings, and considering plot outcomes. Discussion gives an opportunity to build language elaborations as a group and fosters creative thinking.

Modeling

When you first begin to have children retell stories it is essential that you model the task so they know what is expected. This is a critical step for teaching children in a multilinguistic or remedial setting. Most children initially do not know how to approach the retelling task. Use the three-dimensional visuals to pace the story as you model the retelling. After listening to an adult model, children can imitate the standard. Invent and elaborate as you retell the story; this lets children know that they can be creative in the retelling.

Rehearsal

Pair two students for retelling practice. The rehearsal provides opportunities for children to continue to relate, rethink, and make sense of the story. Have the paired students switch roles as listener and reteller; they can get input from each other.

Sharing

Have story retellers share their interpretations with another pair or a small-group audience. Encourage active listening by having the audience watch for features that would enhance their own retelling—voice inflection and volume, pacing, use of pauses, elaborations, and eye contact. First retelling attempts will probably have to be guided with probing questions such as, "Anything else?" Initially, intervene only as much as is necessary for the child to retell a coherent story. Later, make specific suggestions for improvement and ask children to enrich the stories in their own personal ways. Encourage sharing with different audiences, another grade level, or at home.

Follow-Up

Story retelling leads to telling and writing original stories. Such activities stimulate children's powers of creativity and integrate communication skills. For example, *The Jolly Postman or Other People's*

Letters has an envelope slot as the movable, with postal letters that fairy tale characters receive. The book stimulates letter-writing, drawing, and telling other story adventures for the postman.

Conventional books are also used with the six-step strategy and should be included for retelling activities. Three-dimensional prompts are intended to assist children with their initial attempts at story retelling, to interest them in the activity, and to help them be successful.

Resource Bibliography

At the primary level, children need many opportunities to improve their oral language competence and develop a sense of story structure. Story retelling with action book prompts is one way to make listening and speaking an enjoyable and purposeful communication process. Children remember and prize stories they have prepared for retelling.

Use the following bibliography as a guide to help you select action books with appropriate visuals for beginning retellings. As an additional aid, the entries are labeled to indicate the format of the text structure: *W* = Wordless Action Book; *ST* = Simple Text; and *DT* = Developed Story Text.

Ahlberg, Janet, and Allan Ahlberg. *The Jolly Postman or Other People's Letters,* 1986. Boston: Little Brown. ST

All-Action Treasure Hour Pop-Up Books. *Goldilocks and the Three Bears; Jack and the Beanstalk; Puss-in-Boots; Snow White; The Three Little Pigs; Cinderella,* 1983. New York: Outlet Book, Dean's International. DT

Carle, Eric. *The Honeybee and the Robber,* 1981; *The Very Hungry Caterpillar,* 1969. New York: Philomel. ST

DePaola, Tomie. *Giorgio's Village: A Pop-Up Book,* 1982. New York: Putnam. ST

Farris, Stella. *The Magic Blanket,* 1979; *The Magic Bubble Pipe,* 1978; *The Magic Castle,* 1978. New York: Harper and Row. ST

Favorite Tale Pop-Up Books. *Alice in Wonderland; The Three Little Pigs; Cinderella; Tom Thumb; Goldilocks; Puss-in-Boots; The Tortoise and the Hare; The Ugly Duckling,* 1984. New York: Crown. ST

Fowler, Richard. *Mr. Little's Noisy Car,* 1987; *Mr. Little's Noisy Train,* 1987. New York: Grosset and Dunlap. ST

Goodall, John S. *Lavinia's Cottage,* 1981; *Paddy Finds a Job,* 1981; *Shrewbettina Goes to Work,* 1981. New York: Atheneum. W

Gurney, E. *Pop-Up Book of Cats,* 1974; *Pop-Up Book of Dogs,* 1974. New York: Random House. W

Hawkins, Colin, and Jacqui Hawkins. *I Know an Old Lady Who Swallowed a Fly,* 1987; *Old Mother Hubbard,* 1985. New York: Putnam. ST

Hellard, Susan. *Billy Goats Gruff,* 1986; *The Ugly Duckling, 1987. New York: Putnam. ST*

Hill, Eric. Spot Goes to the Beach, 1985; *Spot Goes to the Circus,* 1986; *Where's Spot?,* 1980. New York: Putnam. ST

Hoguet, Susan. *I Unpacked My Grandmother's Trunk,* 1983. New York: Dutton. ST

Koelling, Caryl. *Whose House Is This?,* 1978. Los Angeles: Price/Stern/Sloan. ST

Lustig, Loretta. *The Pop-Up Book of the Circus,* 1976. New York: Random House. W

Pienkowski, Jan. *Dinner Time,* 1984; *Gossip,* 1983; *Little Monsters,* 1986. Los Angeles: Price/Stern/Sloan. ST

Penick, Ib. *Pop-Up Book of Cars,* 1976. New York: Random House. W

Piper, Watty. *The Little Engine That Could: A Pop-Up Book,* 1984. New York: Grosset and Dunlap. DT

Seymour, Peter. *The Animals' Surprise,* 1984. Los Angeles: Price/Stern/Sloan. ST

Shapiro, Arnold. *Squiggly Wiggly's Surprise,* 1978. Los Angeles: Price/Stern/Sloan. ST

Stevenson, James. *Barbara's Birthday,* 1983. New York: Greenwillow. ST

Troll Pop-Up Books. *Cinderella; Paddington's Pop-Up Book; Pinocchio; Snow White and the Seven Dwarfs; Wizard of Oz.* Nahwah, N.J.: Troll Associates. DT

Tudor, Tasha. *Seasons of Delight: A Year on an Old-Fashioned Farm,* 1986. New York: Philomel. W

Wallner, John. *Old MacDonald Had a Farm,* 1986. New York: Dutton. ST

Zoo Pop-Up, 1985. New York: Outlet Book, Dean's International. ST

References

Garnett, Katherine. 1986. Telling Tales: Narratives and Learning-Disabled Children. *Topics in Language Disorders* 6: 44–56.

Goodman, Yetta. 1982. Retellings of Literature and the Comprehension Process. *Theory into Practice* 21: 301–307.

Koskinen, Patricia, *et al.* 1988. Retelling: A Strategy for Enhancing Students' Reading Comprehension. *The Reading Teacher* 41: 892–96.

Morrow, Lesley. 1985. Retelling Stories: A Strategy for Improving Young Children's Comprehension, Concept of Story Structure, and Oral Language Complexity. *The Elementary School Journal* 85: 647–61.

24 Writing Poetry in Response to Literature

Penelope Bryant Turk
Greenfield Junior High School
El Cajon, California

When students discuss literature in the classroom, they are often reluctant to go beyond superficial analysis. When one student has given a response that the teacher accepts enthusiastically, the rest are ready for the next question. They do not feel the need for five "right" answers to an inquiry such as, "What is the theme?" or "Name an outstanding quality of this main character." Writing poetry in response to literature offers the students a variety of reading and writing activities, and the pride students take in sharing their work creates speaking and listening opportunities. Simple pattern poems encourage students to write about setting, character, plot, mood and images, and opposites in the literature they read.

Definition poetry needs nine right answers! Found poetry requires a search through the text for exact details. A cinquain inspires more than one appropriate word to describe a character. A haiku demands not only a consideration of setting but also of mood.

Here are examples of poems written in response to a wide variety of literary selections. Each type of poem is described, examples are given, and directions for writing follow.

Who-What-Where-When-Why Poetry

Who-What-Where-When-Why poetry allows students to summarize the basic elements in any work of literature. For younger children, this assignment would work well as a short-form book report.

The Yearling
The boy Jody
Shot Flag, the Yearling,
At the edge of the sink-hole
On the last day of his boyhood.
A man must "take it for his share
And go on."

Romeo and Juliet
Two star-cross'd lovers
Took their lives
In Capels' monument
One dark and starless night
In continuance of their parents' rage.

Plan of Action

1. Brainstorm answers to the five *W*s.
2. Work the answers into five phrases that seem balanced and pertinent to the work being discussed.
3. Line these up with proper punctuation.
4. Give the work a title that indicates the source.

Haiku to Study Setting

The haiku tries to capture through word imagery the mood or feeling that a scene or natural setting has aroused in the writer. In each of these haiku, note the sensory images.

Arms of fleshlike weed,
Like a nest of octopi . . .
Jungle of Venus.
—"All Summer in a Day"

A deep mountain glen,
A place wild, lonely and shagged . . .
Bed for twenty years.
—"Rip Van Winkle"

Plan of Action

1. Select a key scene from a book in which setting is important.
2. Reread the entire passage or chapter, and make a list of all the words or groups of words that help you visualize the setting.
3. Choose two or three images that are most important to visualizing the setting you have chosen from the book.
4. Arrange your choice of word images in the form of a haiku. Revise and shape your lines until you are satisfied.
5. Remember that a haiku is always written in three lines, counting syllables: five syllables in the first line, seven in the second, and five again in the third.

Cinquain for Characterizations

Cinquain (sin-cane) is an unrhymed form of poetry consisting of five prescribed lines. There are several forms of cinquain floating around, but this is the one I prefer:

Noun
Adjective, adjective
Verb-ing, verb-ing, verb-ing
Four-word free statement
Synonym or equivalent for the topic (noun)

Goldilocks
Curious, adventurous
Sitting, eating, sleeping
A rather unbearable child
Visitor

Anne
Introspective, philosophical
Writing, growing, dreaming
Memorialized in a diary
Victim

Plan of Action

1. Pick a subject from literature.
2. Brainstorm a list of adjectives for this character.
3. Brainstorm a list of present participles to show action.
4. Brainstorm a list of synonyms for this character; now write!

Acrostic Poetry to Summarize Plot

In an acrostic poem the title (topic) is printed vertically, letter by letter. Each letter is used in the construction of phrases or sentences to describe the topic.

Snow White
Never should have touched that
Old apple! The
Wicked
Witch
Had her enchanted, but
In stepped
The prince and they lived happily
Ever after.

Wilting in
A
Life of
Torment, Walter
Eased out of
Reality.

Maybe
It was
The only way
To stay
Young and heroic.

Plan of Action

1. Choose a title, preferably not too long.
2. Brainstorm words that start with the appropriate letters.
3. If sustained phrases are too difficult, try this kind of poetry to analyze setting or character.

Found Poetry to Focus on Effect

Found poetry is aptly named inasmuch as it consists of creating a poem by selecting lines from an already existing work of literature. This is a good way to get the students to focus on a particular stylistic device, such as similes or metaphors, on a particular theme, symbol, or image.

"Telltale Heart"—Poe
Very, very dreadfully nervous,
I heard many things in hell:
The groan of mortal terror,
A ringing in my ears,
A low dull sound,
Low stifled sound,
A mockery of my horror!
Hellish tattoo!
Louder! Louder! Louder! Louder!
The beating of his hideous heart!

Plan of Action

1. Have students list on paper all the phrases that lend themselves to a particular effect.
2. Select those that work and rearrange them appropriately.

Diamante to Explore Opposites

A close cousin of the cinquain is the form of unrhymed poetry called the diamante. Because of its physical appearance on paper, it was christened with the Italian word for *diamond.* It is often used to explore opposites and works well when the class is studying a dramatic change in a literary persona's character or is comparing two characters who are complete opposites.

Cinderella
Orphan
Poor, lonely
Sweeping, scrubbing, longing
Stepmother, kitchen,—Ballroom, godmother
Dancing, loving, winning
Happy, enchanted
Princess

A Tale of Two Cities
Best of Times
Faithful, hopeful
Working, wanting, awaking
Light, wisdom,—foolishness, Darkness
Spending, stirring, sliding
Incredulous, desperate
Worst of Times

Plan of Action

1. Name the topic noun (first line).
2. Decide on the antonym (last line).
3. Select two describing words for topic noun and two for antonym.
4. Generate three action words for topic noun and three for antonym.
5. Decide on four words (nouns are best), two of which fit the topic noun and two of which fit the antonym.
6. Put them together in the following pattern:

Topic (noun)
Two describing words (adjectives)
Three action words (*-ing* form)
Two words to capture topic—two words to capture antonym
Three action words for ending noun
Two describing words for ending noun
Ending noun (antonym)

Definition Poetry

Definition poetry is a form of free verse that uses a selection of succinct phrases to define an idea or concept. It is important to encourage picturesque, sensitive phrases that are brief and have a good balance of images and expressions of feeling.

What have you learned?
  Work together
  Build to last
  Do it right
  Make it good
  Lock the door
  Distrust strangers
  Listen for huffing
  Beware of wolves
  Suffer the consequences
That's what we've learned.

—"The Three Little Pigs"

What is Cold?
  A subtle gloom
  Absence of sun
  All pure white
  Spittle crackling in air
  Seventy-five below
  Fine powder of frost
  Numbness of fingers
  Hands like weights
  Sentence of death
That is Cold!

—Jack London's "To Build a Fire"

Plan of Action

1. Select a topic appropriate to the work being studied. The topic could have to do with setting, character, theme, symbol, or stylistic devices.
2. Brainstorm phrases that fit the topic.
3. Arrange these in an effective manner, keeping tone and rhythm in mind.
4. Add the introductory and concluding lines at the margin. The other lines are all indented. Usually no more than nine phrases are used.

25 Style from the Inside Out

Patricia P. Kelly
Virginia Tech

Anyone who has tried to teach the concept of literary style has watched students' eyes glaze over when confronted with an illuminating definition, such as, "Style is a writer's characteristic manner of expression, the unique arrangement of words and structures that distinguish one writer from another." The frustration hangs thick in the air, a result of dealing with such an abstract concept from the "outside," by looking in, analyzing, tearing apart. I had quickly abandoned that approach, of course, but despite many variations in teaching strategies, both my students and I had struggled so unsuccessfully with the concept of literary style that I had either to find a way to put the students into the author's role, where they would go inside the author's style and manipulate language and structures in the manner of that author, or abandon the effort entirely.

In desperation I settled on a strategy called *imitation* (Weathers and Winchester 1978). I also remembered that in his *Autobiography,* Benjamin Franklin discusses learning to write by copying selected passages from various sources and writing in the style of those authors. The first time I used imitation, I watched students frown, look puzzled, chew their pencils, and scribble; but most memorable were the satisfied smiles when they boldly placed the last period and lifted their pencils triumphantly. Then came the silent sharing of papers as they passed their work around while others finished. The students were proud of their papers, but they also wanted to see what others had done, how others had perhaps solved particular stylistic problems. As students shared orally, they all agreed their papers "sounded good," and they asked to try it again.

The selection of literature to imitate is perhaps the most critical step in the process. I choose sentences or paragraphs from works we are studying, or sometimes whole pieces, particularly short, unrhymed poems, that I think will make good models and that students will enjoy playing with. I first read the model aloud so that students hear the rhythm of the structures. Students then write an exact copy of the original in their own handwriting. In this way they feel the rhythm of the structures as they write them. We discuss possible topics that might fit with the model, and students then choose subjects, distinct and different from the model. They write their own pieces with this new subject, trying to make their piece sound like the original with its general manner and style, structure and syntax, and rhythm.

My directions to the students emphasize the notion of just sounding similar to the original, even though they often change the tone from serious to humorous. In these *loose imitations,* students may vary from the original syntax by omitting certain structures or adding additional ones. Usually I have introduced the concept of imitation by putting a sentence such as, "Clanging loudly, the fire engine raced down the dark street," on the board, and we have followed the process as a group. The model below, from *Roll of Thunder, Hear My Cry,* is followed by an example of a student's loose imitation, a first draft written in class.

> Spring. It seeped unseen into the waiting red earth in early March, softening the hard ground for the coming plow and awakening life that had lain gently sleeping through the cold winter. But by the end of March it was evident everywhere: in the barn where three new calves bellowed and chicks the color of soft pale sunlight chirped and in the yard where the wisteria and English dogwood bushes readied themselves for their annual Easter bloom . . . (Taylor 1976, 148)
>
> Sadness. It seeped unfelt into the solitary blonde girl in early evening, entering the dark room in the quiet home and awakening thoughts that had lain gently sleeping through the busy day. But by the end of evening it was evident everywhere: in her eyes where two tears appeared and lips the color of hard red rubies trembled and in her helpless manner where her hands and arms fluttered in the darkness.

The exactness of the imitation is not as important as the process. Students are writing structures they would not write naturally; they are experimenting with another writer's style by "trying on those unique trappings" of a particular author that essentially constitute his or her literary style. Sometimes I conclude the process with sharing and a general acknowledgment of the students' success. If the model contains some challenging structures, I often put a copy on the overhead and have students talk about ways they solved some of the difficult places. Such class discussions provide ways of talking about style from the "inside out" and also model for students some ways of talking about writing in their groups.

First-draft, loose imitations provide excellent opportunities for writing groups to look closely at the language and structure that constitute style. Unlike a writing-group situation where four different papers with differing organizational patterns and varying degrees of problems must be dealt with, in these discussions, student writers have struggled with the same forms and know what they did to solve the problems. As students read their drafts, the writing-group members follow the original model, checking places where the rhythm and structure vary greatly. Students start the discussion of their papers by identifying the area where the imitation "just doesn't sound right."

Our writer decided that the imitation fell apart in the last sentence, so the group concentrated its efforts there. The group decided to drop *helpless* because it had no counterpart in the original and because such a "telling" word added nothing to the description. The model's *English dogwood bushes* became *slender porcelain hands* after much discussion of syllables, proper nouns, tone, and meaning. The evolution of the last prepositional was interesting to watch. The writer did not like her last phrase at all, and the group decided rather quickly to change it to *for their nightly sweet song.* After making some changes in the second sentence, one student said that the last phrase "just isn't right even though it has the same rhythm." The phrase eventually became *sweet night song,* but then a student noted that the words *tears* and *trembled* seemed to indicate *bittersweet,* and the phrase became *bittersweet night song.* The group was satisfied with the imitation although some variations from the original remained.

After this intense discussion and reworking in a writing group, the student draft below more nearly approximates a *close imitation,* where the new topic is put into structures that follow as nearly as possible the syntax and phrasing of the original writer.

> Sadness. It seeped unfelt into the solitary blonde girl in early evening, entering the quiet room in the darkening home and awakening thoughts that had been silently gathering through the busy day. But by the end of evening it was evident everywhere: in her eyes where two bright tears appeared and lips the color of hard red rubies trembled and in her manner where her body and slender porcelain hands busied themselves at the piano for their bittersweet night song.

Both in the whole-class and small-group discussions of their imitations, students are indirectly asking evaluative questions, such as: Does it sound like the original? Are the structures similar? Is it the same form of word? Does it make sense? They are talking about the interaction among language and meaning and style. By making students producers of literature, we can make them better consumers of literature, because linking those processes can only complement the learning of each.

References

Taylor, Mildred D. 1976. *Roll of Thunder, Hear My Cry.* New York: Bantam.

Weathers, Winston, and Otis Winchester. 1978. *The New Strategy of Style.* New York: McGraw-Hill.

26 Creating Text: Students Connecting with Literature

Leila Christenbury
Virginia Commonwealth University

For many of our students, the creation of literature is an arcane science that is also, many of them feel, a fairly painless process. Students often feel that ideas come quickly to writers, that their writing is rarely revised, and that a writer's feelings about a work once it is published are uniformly positive.

Students don't know—and teachers often forget to remind them—about the wrenching struggle that writers go through to create. We hear from writers' accounts of their own lives of their not infrequent battle to get initial ideas, severe writers' block in the middle of writing, and a frequent loss of faith about the utility of the entire process itself. Dorothy Parker, wit and American writer, lightly but perceptively sums it up: "I love having written."

In the classroom it can be helpful to remind students that real writers often lose half or more of their work in revisions (we think of poet T. S. Eliot and novelist Thomas Wolfe). It may be useful to tell the story, perhaps more true than apocryphal, of novelist Henry James spending all morning putting a word in and all afternoon taking it out; of the writer Honoré de Balzac, writing standing up in late-night sessions and using the scissors attached to his waist to literally cut apart his manuscripts, leaving heaps of paper strips on the floor.

After publication, writers can still feel ambiguous about their writing. Students might be interested to know that writer Paule Marshall often changes her own published work as she reads it aloud to audiences, revising what is in print because she is never satisfied with it. Some students will know that John Fowles wrote and published two versions of his novel *The Magus,* and some may have heard of the occasional writer who entirely disclaims a piece of work once in print.

Beyond these stories of real writers and their writing, how do we get our students to see literature as a truly creative activity, filled with starts and stops and crises of confidence?

Clearly, if all we have our students do is discuss a printed text, which often by its very appearance implies permanence and inevitability, they will treat the text with a reverence that makes them more a spectator of literature. Joseph Williams (1987) of the University of Chicago's English department describes such an attitude as "admiring the monuments," not really participating in literature, and surely not connecting with it. While Arthur N. Applebee, looking at James Britton's work, sees the advantages of such a spectator stance ("in this role we are removed from the demands of direct involvement . . . to establish ourselves in the spectator role is to establish the conviction that we do not have to act as the result of our experience" [1985, 90]), there are drawbacks.

Ben Nelms, writing in *Literature in the Classroom* (1988), sees text as "the blueprint around which all activity at a construction site is centered" (1). Too much of watching others build only convinces students that "they could never do the same thing"—what students need, Nelms feels, is not just to stare through the wire fence at the construction site but to build themselves, to create text. The philosophy of reader-response demands a similar connection of students and text, and Louise Rosenblatt in *Literature as Exploration* (1938) notes, "One of the best ways of helping students to gain this appreciation of literary form and artistry is to encourage them to engage in . . . imaginative writing. In this way they will themselves be involved in wrestling with the materials" (148).

Creation of text, where students write their own literature—based on literature—is a powerful way to connect students with literature:

- creating text is inventive as students are writing literature;
- creating text is skill-based as students are writing;
- creating text relates to literary criticism as students, by writing literature, are writing about literature.

A few teaching principles for creating text are in order. The following seven are helpful in preparing students to create text (1, 2), choosing appropriate literature from which the text is based (3, 4), creating the text itself (5), and assessing the created text (6, 7).

1. As a pre-activity to creating text, students need brief exposure to the world of real writers—who struggle for ideas; revise multiple drafts; and who, even after a work is in print, often feel ambivalent about the "finished" product. Sharing stories of professional writers and sharing your own drafts will help set the stage for creating text.

2. While students do not need to discuss or thoroughly examine a piece of literature before they create text, they do need to have a basic grasp of the concepts of plot, setting, character, and theme.
3. Students need to read and create text from accessible (i.e., interesting, understandable) pieces of literature.
4. The piece of literature should be compact; short stories are ideal.
5. Students should create short pieces of text. Longer pieces can seem overwhelming to students.
6. Have multiple copies of the original piece of literature available so students can cut and paste their own versions in, before, or after the piece. The examination/assessment of isolated beginnings, endings, or interleaved paragraphs are less effective out of context.
7. Students need, after the creation of text, to assess their work on its own terms *and* in relation to the original. They need to think not in terms of better or worse but in terms of differences, choices, options.

Although students may be willing, even eager, to create text once they are prepared and have an appropriate piece of literature, they need direction as to what part or parts of the literature can be manipulated, modeled, changed. In short, students need guidance or "ways in" to connect themselves with literature.

This outline may help. While the activities and headings are fairly arbitrary, they provide a starting point for the student.

I. Plot
   A. Change Scenes
      1. Add character(s)
      2. Delete character(s)
      3. Change dialogue (e.g., crucial word/key phrase)
      4. Identify high point (climax) and rewrite
   B. Change Ending
      1. Write new ending
      2. Extend ending in time (hour/day/week/month/year) and write sequel
   C. Change Beginning
      1. Write new beginning
      2. Extend beginning in time (hour/day/week/month/year) and write prequel

D. Change Title
  1. Rewrite opening paragraph to reflect new title
  2. Rewrite closing paragraph to reflect new title

II. Setting
  A. Change era
  B. Change locale
  C. Change time of year/time of day

III. Character
  A. Rename character(s)
  B. Change sex of character(s)
  C. Change major personality trait(s) of character(s)
  D. Change major physical characteristic(s) of character(s)

Even with such a list, however, some students may need more specific direction. The following is a list of activities for creating text based on a short story, Todd Strasser's "On the Bridge," found in *Visions,* edited by Donald R. Gallo (1987). "On the Bridge" is a tight and well-structured piece that features two teenage protagonists and a clear conflict. While, again, the categories and activities are somewhat arbitrary, they provide a starting place for students who have read "On the Bridge" to create alternative text.

I. Plot
  A. Change Scenes

—Rewrite the scene on p. 125 to:	The woman in the blue Toyota crashes; *or*
	The woman in the blue Toyota calls the cops and they appear.
—Rewrite the scene on p. 124 to:	The trucker blasts back his horn at Seth.
—If the high point or climax is on pp. 126–27, have:	Adam take the blame for the incident and rewrite the climax; *or*
	Seth lick off the cigarette ash and rewrite the climax.

  B. Change Ending

—Rewrite the scene on p. 128 to:	Seth keeps the jacket; *or*
	Adam apologizes to Seth.
—Extend the scene on p. 128 to:	A week later; *or*
	Three months later; *or*
	Two years later.

(What is Adam up to? Seth? What is the state of their friendship? What does Adam wear? Seth?)

C. Title
—Rewrite the opening paragraph with the title "The Jacket."

II. Setting
—Change the location from an interstate bridge to a shopping center crosswalk/bridge. Then rewrite any two incidents.

III. Character
—Change Seth and Adam to Marcy and Liz and rewrite any significant dialogue.
—Change the three guys in the nylon suits (pp. 125–27) to:
A young couple in their 20s; *or*
An older man; *or*
A feisty middle-aged woman.

Some students may not wish to consider creating as many text alternatives as this above offers. For those students, it is possible to narrow down the options. Using Colby Rodowsky's "Amanda and the Wounded Birds," from the same collection (Gallo 1987), a teacher can present students with a more focused direction.

Choose One.

1. Rewrite the opening of "Amanda" (p. 78) and change Amanda's mother's job; make the mother divorced, not widowed; change the mother to a father. Write one paragraph to reflect the changes.
2. Alter the scene on p. 85 when Amanda and her mother go to lunch. Make the lunch a strained, halting affair and include Amanda's thoughts. Write three to five paragraphs to reflect these changes.
3. Change Amanda to Aaron and rewrite her problems (p. 81) to reflect his problems. Write two paragraphs.

Once students have made literature, have created text, they are in a better position to assess it and to connect with it. They need no longer hang around the construction site, admiring what others build—they can invent, forge, make on their own. Once we can help students participate in literature by actually creating it, we empower them and make ever stronger their connection to the language arts.

References

Applebee, Arthur N. 1985. Studies in the Spectator Role: An Approach to Response to Literature. In *Researching Response to Literature and the Teaching of Literature,* edited by Charles R. Cooper. Norwood, N.J.: Ablex.

Gallo, Donald R., editor. 1987. *Visions.* New York: Delacorte.

Nelms, Ben, editor. 1988. *Literature in the Classroom: Readers, Texts, and Contexts.* Urbana, Ill.: National Council of Teachers of English.

Rosenblatt, Louise. 1938. *Literature as Exploration, for the Commission on Human Relations.* New York: Noble and Noble.

Williams, Joseph. 1987. Critical Thinking vs. Acquiring Knowledge or, On Doing More than Admiring the Monuments. Speech delivered at the annual conference of the Virginia Association of Teachers of English.

27 Helping Students Discover Their Private Texts

Leroy Perkins
University of Alaska—Fairbanks

In the past, I prepared periodic essay exams on assigned readings (fiction and nonfiction, poetry, and drama) for freshman and sophomore college composition and introduction to literature courses. To write these exams, I would pluck passages I deemed "important" from the readings and frame questions around them. Questions like, "Identify and discuss levels of irony in Ozymandias' injunction to 'Look on my works, ye Mighty, and despair!' " Or, "Illustrate how Charley's graveside observation that 'No man only needs a little salary' applies to your understanding of major themes in *Death of a Salesman.*" Or, "Analyze why Hawthorne describes Goodman Brown as 'himself the chief horror of the scene'." Eventually, I got bored juggling exam lingo: *identify, illustrate, analyze, discuss, compare.* All these words added up to pretty much the same thing: "Say something interesting about this passage."

For a year or two I gave up the pretense of trying to make questions sound different and just provided students with a list of quotes to write about. But I began to wonder why *I* should be the one to decide what parts of the text are important. Why not let the students choose? Thinking about this quesiton led to a classroom procedure that encourages students to find personal relevance in literature as a means of examining their lives and their values. While I have employed this exercise only in the college classroom, I think it would also be appropriate for literature classes at earlier levels in the curriculum.

Teachers who use reader-response theory to help students select and develop topics for what eventually become formal papers encourage students to highlight passages in their reading that speak loudly *for them.* To make class discussions and students' writing less teacher-centered, I've developed the following scenario, which I follow once a week or so for a class that meets three times weekly:

1. Students read the assigned pages (which often include more than one work) and select two quotations from the reading that they would like to write about or think would give someone else lots to write about. I do the same.
2. Students write their quotations on half-sheets of paper, indicating where the quotation came from (including the page number). Students put their names on each half-sheet and prepare them as part of their homework. I do the same.
3. As a prewriting warm-up, the students and I talk in general terms about our homework reading experiences (surprises, questions, likes, and dislikes).
4. Students divide their quotations into two piles (to avoid the possible congestion of one) on desks in the center of our discussion circle. Mine go there too.
5. Students gather around the piles (I call them "bonfires," for no good reason) and take five minutes to select a quotation they would like to write about. They may pick any quotation they choose, *as long as it is not their own.* I ask students to return the quotation they've chosen to one of the piles, so another student may choose it. I pick a quotation, too. The proviso that students cannot respond to their own quotation insures that students will not come to class with a canned essay to copy. The proviso encourages students to complete the assigned reading, much as a quiz would do, without a quiz's evaluative overtones. This ploy also encourages students to think about what they have read before coming to class, so that they have a ready stock of ideas to match whatever passage they choose to write about. Thus students develop abilities to think and write extemporaneously, a skill they will need for essay examinations in other courses.
6. Students freewrite (Peter Elbow's term) for ten minutes or so on the quotation they have chosen. Their objective is to get as much as they can on paper, without fussing over spelling, punctuation, and grammar. I write as well, usually on the board. Students know that this is not a "test," that the objective is to build writing fluency. Following Elbow's suggestion, I announce in advance whether students will be writing for themselves alone, or will later read their pieces aloud in small groups, and/or will hand their pieces in for me to read, *but not to grade.* Thus students write for audiences that gradually become more public. Early in the term, students write for

themselves in reading-response journals, in learning logs, or during in-class exercises such as the one I have described. Later, students write drafts for each other, for me, and eventually for an outside reader.

7. I read aloud the piece I have just written, and I then lead a brief discussion about what I've said and how I've said it. This is an excellent opportunity to discuss rhetorical strategies, as well as for students to develop an ear for rhythms in the language. Some days I please myself with what I write and some days I flop, and the latter instances seem to be especially gratifying and instructive for students. Once students and I have established a cordial classroom atmosphere, I encourage volunteers to "play teacher," and some students take me up on it, writing on the board, reading aloud, and discussing their writing process.
8. Students read their pieces aloud in small groups (no more than four students per group), commenting on each other's writing as both responses to the literature and as samples of rhetoric in context. Early in the semester I ask students to say only positive things about each other's writing, such as "I like the way you . . ." Later on, students may also make more critical comments, such as "I wish you had said more about . . ." While the groups are working, I try to keep four or five ears open at once, listening in and occasionally commenting.
9. Students in each group select one or two of their papers to read aloud to the class as a whole (if there is time).
10. I gather the quotations from the center piles and check them off after class, indicating the student has done the assignment. Sometimes I will comment on a quotation, but never critically. About a third of the time, I ask students to hand in the pieces they have written. I read these only to check on students' fluency, and to comment on ideas that might prove fruitful in students' subsequent drafts. One of the main purposes of the exercise is to give students material they can later develop into formal papers.

Yes, it's possible to do all this in an hour. But the prewriting discussion must be brief. I devote other class periods to more prolonged discussions of the texts, to ten-minute writing "bursts" on topics that come up in our discussions, and to workshops in which students help each other select and develop paper topics, depending how far along students are on their drafts.

The exercise I've described is consistent with our department's composition guidelines, which require that students write in every class. Additionally, the exercise fosters relatively low-pressure writing experiences—there is enough "writing as test" elsewhere in the curriculum. Students need every opportunity to "worry a point," to write out their ideas in a nonjudgmental context. Because I believe students should have many chances to do their best work as they take their writing through multiple drafts, I stopped giving exams altogether, since it makes no sense to evaluate what Donald Murray calls "discovery drafts."

In identifying and responding to what they see as potentially fertile passages, students create private versions of the texts they read, texts in which some parts are more important than others. The exercise I have described nudges students to go public with their private texts—the portions of the assigned reading they highlight. The student-selected quotations often tell me something about how well students are reading and indicate the level of students' ability to abstract key ideas from their texts. I use this information in organizing future class discussions. This exercise also gives students a way to help each other become more attentive readers by having students draw attention to portions of the reading that their peers may have overlooked. But what I like best about this exercise is the way it puts students in control of deciding which passages in our common texts might prove most fruitful for further thinking and writing.

28 An Approach to Critical Writing: Begin with Contradictions

Janet Bean-Thompson
University of New Hampshire

"So you want us to look out for curveballs," said a student in my freshman writing class.

We were talking about critical essays, not baseball, so Paul's comment surprised me at first. I had asked my students to respond to problems they encountered in the text—an unexpected detail, a contradiction in a character's actions, a confusing passage, or a cryptic metaphor. But Paul's baseball metaphor made more sense to the class than anything I had said. Everyone had seen a pitcher throw a curveball; now they could watch for an author to throw one, too.

Too often, inexperienced writers avoid writing about the things that confuse them. Fearing the ambiguous, they overlook troublesome passages in favor of easy generalizations. They feel they have enough problems with reading without creating more for themselves. Unfortunately, this approach can lead to dull, lifeless essays.

Reading critically is hard work. In his essay, "Coming to Words," Gary Lindberg writes: "To comprehend what is written requires the same trial-and-error process that produced the writing in the first place" (1986, 152). Comprehension, according to Lindberg, comes from changes in reading: shifts in patterns, misreadings, unexpected details, disruptions, or apparent contradictions. Before we can teach our students to write critical analyses, we must help them understand that reading, like writing, is a process. Meaning is not "hidden" in the text; it comes from within. To begin the process of understanding, every reader must start at the point of confusion.

If I extend my student's baseball metaphor, the point of confusion would be directly behind homeplate, watching for the author's curveballs. But most students don't squat behind the plate ready for the pitch; they sit in the last row of the stadium munching a hot dog. If asked to analyze the game, they notice a pattern and generalize. For example, they might assert that accurate throwing is important to the game. For the next few innings, they look for support—a good throw that caused a double play or an overthrow that allowed a run. The generalization is valid—but who would argue that throwing is *not* important?

Essays about literature often work the same way: students notice a pattern, generalize, then find specific support. We have all seen essays like this—flawless in design, but missing something essential. Before they can write meaningful essays, students must engage in the struggle to create meaning. Bartholomae and Petrosky identify the crux of the problem:

> [M]eaning becomes something external, something contained in a text (the way a can of peas contains peas), or something that exists out in the world (like a chair or a desk), rather than something that results when a reader or writer finds language to make the presentation of meaning possible . . . (1986, 11).

Baseball players cannot understand the game by sitting in the stadium, and readers cannot find meaning until they struggle to create it from within.

When asked to write a critical essay, most students begin with external "truths" rather than with the text. They take conventional wisdom—"hardships force you to grow up," "good always wins out over evil," or "love is more important than money"—and apply these ready-made interpretations to the text. While the specifics of a novel or story might support such an interpretation, the analysis will almost always be dull. The reader did not create meaning; he or she merely borrowed empty phrases.

Readers need an alternative to this general-to-specific approach. As my students read Maya Angelou's *I Know Why the Caged Bird Sings* (1970), I gave two writing assignments designed to encourage a specific-to-general approach. In their journals, I had them jot down patterns, questions, unexpected details, and the page numbers of confusing passages. Next, they wrote a short essay about the first half of the book, using their journals for ideas. Despite the fact that they had a wealth of specifics in their journals, many students still relied on the general-to-specific approach. My second writing assignment *forced* them to begin with specifics. I asked them to select a short, troubling passage—a curveball—and write it at the top of their paper. In their essays, they discussed the problems they had with the passage and the solutions they came up with. Because the reading process was part of the assignment, my students experimented, struggled, and wrote insightful essays.

There was a strong contrast between the first essays, which began with generalizations, and the second essays, which began with specifics. While the first essays supported obvious theses, the second group raised important questions. Many of the first essays were plodding and dull, but the second essays were full of lively academic inquiry. I will use exerpts from four students' essays to show the difference a specific-to-general approach can make.

Chris, like most of the class, began his first essay with a generalization:

> In the book *I Know Why the Caged Bird Sings* the theme of religion is found throughout the storyline. During the story religion is always involved in Maya's life and is brought to her through her grandmother who she called "Mamma."

The first paragraph establishes the obvious fact that religion is important, but Chris makes no attempt to explain why or how it is important. Instead, he lapses into repetition. The rest of Chris's essay shows that he knows the formula for a well-organized essay. Each paragraph begins with a key phrase:

> "One example of religion . . ."
>
> "There were other ways religion was in their lives."
>
> "One important example of religion . . ."

Chris probably followed the formula his high school teacher taught him: Introduction with a thesis, three paragraphs with examples, and a conclusion. The essay has structure, but it lacks substance.

In his second essay, however, Chris tackled a difficult problem concerning religion. He selected a quote and explained why it surprised him:

> "Of course, I knew God was white too, but no one could have made me believe he was prejudiced" (p. 40).
>
> The idea that a little black girl who was surrounded by black people and practiced her religion everyday with other black people could think that her God was white seems a little different than what a person might expect. The first impression a person might get would be a black person's God is black and a white person's God is white. . . . If whitefolk were prejudiced towards blacks all the time, then why wouldn't God, who is white in Maya's eyes, be prejudiced too?

Even if Chris cannot answer all the questions he has raised, at least he is asking the right kind of questions. He discusses how the quote challenged his expectations, and he sees the implicit contradiction in

God being both white and unprejudiced. By finding problems, he has begun the process of understanding.

Like Chris, Charlie began his first essay with a generalization: "Maya Angelou is a young black girl whose life is one way or another hung up with guilt." He also knew the formula of the five-paragraph essay: introduction, three supporting paragraphs, and conclusion. While most people would agree that his thesis and support are valid, no one would applaud his originality. Yet given the assignment to find a curveball, Charlie found an unfamiliar word, researched it, and wrote an interesting character study. His essay began:

> "Mother and Bailey were entangled in the Oedipal Skein. Neither could live with or without the other" (p. 218).
>
> When I think of a mother/son relationship, the words love, understanding, and sympathy come to mind. A son naturally looks to his mother for advice, warmth, encouragement, and also just someone to talk to . . . but Bailey's relationship with his mother is a much different one.

When Charlie handed in his essay, he asked me, "Have you ever heard of this Oedipal stuff before?" He was proud of his discovery—and eager to share his knowledge with me. I almost did not want to tell him I knew who Freud was. Using what he learned about the Oedipus complex, he analyzed Bailey's character. He explored *why* the characters behave the way they do:

> Bailey's resentment toward his mother that he felt earlier had just slipped away from him. While Maya was ripping her hair out trying to answer the question like why did they send us away? And what did we do wrong? Bailey was just burying his resentment toward her deep in his heart, letting love and fascination overwhelm it.

Charlie was proud of his essay because he—not the teacher—created meaning. Like others in my class, he felt a sense of mastery that was not present before.

While writing their curveball essays, many students discovered the importance of rereading and analyzing their reactions. Ellen kept returning to a chapter that surprised and disgusted her:

> When first reading this chapter, I was shocked to see that Maya seemed to be defending the black's bigotry against the Japanese and other Orientals. The author, who had earlier in her novel condemned the actions of anyone who acted against her people because of their color, appeared to be condoning similar racist behavior by the Negroes.
>
> Upon further consideration and a few more readings, however, it became progressively clearer that Maya was not really

> attempting a defense of their actions. Instead, she was using shallow, sometimes sarcastic arguments and sharp words to show how ridiculous this self-defeating behavior was.

Once Ellen identified an apparent contradiction, she had to look beyond the obvious to make meaning. How could Angelou say one thing and mean another? Ellen resolved this conflict by looking at the narrator:

> Maya Angelou used two different tones or "voices" to get her point across to the readers. The first voice was herself as a child, innocent and almost completely oblivious to the happenings and wrongdoings in the world. The second was Maya the adult, looking back.

Instead of accepting the words of the narrator as truth, Ellen challenged the text, looking for meaning that made sense *to her.* By seeing layers of meaning in the text, Ellen has begun to understand the power and potential of literature.

Even with basic writers, this assignment encouraged higher-level thinking. Tony had never written a critical analysis before, but his essay shows insight and close reading. He chose a metaphor as his curveball:

> "I was a loose kite in a gentle wind floating with only my will for an anchor" (p. 214).
>
> I believe this statement is kind of a tricky one to decipher. I think a logical explanation could be that Maya is caught between a thin line. I mean that she is battling two sides of feelings. I think that Maya does not want to be alone in the world. But on the other hand she has the need to be a survivor.

Tony, seeing the contradiction in the freedom of the kite and the steadiness of an anchor, found a parallel contradiction in Maya's feelings. Although he felt Angelou's autobiography was difficult to "decipher," he could create meaning by analyzing a problem.

A certain level of sophistication is inherent in this writing assignment: a specific problem must be identified and solved. Essays that begin with easy generalizations lead students to hunt through the text for suppport; essays that begin with problems challenge students to think through the reading process. The curveball essay avoids many of the problems students usually have with critical writing. Because students write a specific quote at the top of their essays, their thoughts are already focused. Since they must work with direct quotes, their essays aren't vague. Most importantly, the assignment triggers analysis. Students solve their own problems—and create their own meanings.

References

Angelou, M. 1970. *I Know Why the Caged Bird Sings.* New York: Bantam.

Bartholomae, D., and A. Petrosky. 1986. *Facts, Artifacts, and Counterfacts: Theory and Method for a Reading and Writing Course.* Upper Montclair, N.J.: Boynton/Cook.

Lindberg, G. 1986. Coming to Words: Writing as Process and the Reading of Literature. In *Only Connect: Uniting Reading and Writing,* edited by T. Newkirk. Upper Montclair, N.J.: Boynton/Cook.

Editor

Patricia Phelan is chair of the Classroom Practices Committee of NCTE. She is a teacher-leader in the California Literature Project, a Chapter One Reading Resource teacher at Crawford High School in San Diego, and an adjunct professor of English at Miramar Community College. A fellow in the San Diego Area Writing Project and the Humanities Institute, she has degrees in political science, English, and education. She has written curriculum for her school district, contributed to a language arts textbook, and published in *English Journal* and NCTE affiliate journals.

Titles in the Classroom Practices in Teaching English Series

NCTE began publishing the Classroom Practices series in 1963 with *Promising Practices in the Teaching of English.* Volumes 1–16 and Volume 18 of the series are out of print. The following titles are available through the NCTE *Catalog.*

Vol.	*Title*
17.	How to Handle the Paper Load (1979)
19.	Structuring for Success in the English Classroom (1982)
20.	Non-native and Nonstandard Dialect Students (1982)
21.	Literature—News That Stays News: Fresh Approaches to the Classics (1985)
22.	Activities to Promote Critical Thinking (1986)
23.	Focus on Collaborative Learning (1988)
24.	Talking to Learn (1989)
25.	Literature and Life: Making Connections in the Classroom (1990)